The Soaps

SCENE
STEALING SCENES
FOR ACTORS

The Soaps

SCENE
STEALING SCENES
FOR ACTORS

Karen Dent

MERIWETHER PUBLISHING LTD.
Colorado Springs, Colorado

PN
2080
.D46
1989
Feb 2002
A BN3569

Meriwether Publishing Ltd., Publisher
P.O. Box 7710
Colorado Springs, CO 80933

Editor: Arthur Zapel
Typesetting: Cheryl Tuder
Cover design: K. Anne Kircher

© Copyright MCMLXXXIX Meriwether Publishing Ltd.
Printed in the United States of America
First Edition

Library of Congress Cataloging-in-Publication Data

Dent, Karen.
  The soaps : scene stealing scenes for actors / Karen Dent.
      p.   cm.
  ISBN 0-916260-60-7
  1. Acting.   2. Soap operas.   I. Title.
PN2080.D46   1989
812'.02508--dc20   89-37760
                                                            CIP

This book is dedicated to Bob Adler who has loved, nurtured and supported me through all I've been through; to my mom, Eileen, who has always believed in me and who has given of her time and experience to help me reach my goals; to my sister, Roxanne, my best friend and loudest supporter; to Russ Weatherford, my teacher and friend; and of course to you, the Actor, who tries so hard and gives so much — this one's for you.

CONTENTS

CONTENTS (cont.)

PART 3: MAN AND WOMAN

A Word from the Author

These scenes have all been performed "on camera" in situations which grew out of a production/soap technique class started in New York City. Being an actress in the class I started writing my own scenes, ones which I felt better represented who I was and what I wanted to convey.

They were a success and so many people began to seek me out asking for scenes that were both original and specifically written for their "type." When they auditioned for casting directors or agents, they offered to pay me for special scenes just for them.

That kind of support and encouragement was overwhelming and was the beginning of my idea to share some of my best scenes, in book form with you.

Being first an actress, I understand how tough it is to look for and find that special scene that's just right for you. My characters are real, with human reactions to problems that are not necessarily off the wall, though highly charged with the passion that is necessary for auditions. I love to use humor and incorporate it whenever I can. While these scenes are short enough to hold interest they are also long enough to have substance.

I hope you enjoy them as much as I enjoyed writing them.

Break a leg!

Karen Dent
New York City

INTRODUCTION

The purpose of the "close-out" soap scene is to catch the viewers and intrigue them enough so that they stay tuned to the program. The purpose of an audition piece is to make the casting director or agent stay tuned to you and your career and find a program suited to your talents and abilities. These scenes will definitely give you the edge you need in capturing their attention and make them take notice for the short time usually allotted to you.

These scenes were written expressly for a Soap Production class, led by Russ Weatherford which was held in New York City at AIA. They were all tested in on-camera situations and were modified and changed to suit that medium. They can be used for some over-the-shoulder shots and be used with very little movement, which is necessary for film work. Nowadays, there is a great call for actors to bring in a tape of their work. This originally started in California but has moved steadily to the East Coast where agents and casting directors here also find it helpful. While these were written with the eye of the camera in mind, they also lend themselves beautifully to any kind of audition situation; theatre, film, tape or class work. Although they were written specifically with the impact of a "close-out" in mind, this actually adds to the scenes' abilities to make the actor stand out.

Soap scenes by nature are of conflict and drama. That's why, when commanding the audience's attention, they can justify so many dramatic situations where the characters are either black or white, good or bad. But the stories also have to be believable and the people have to have some shadings of grey, otherwise they become cardboard characters.

These scenes have that and more. They have passion. Each character has a story and a point of view to tell, which is important. That way, no one will be "cheated" if they play the other guy.

Actors know that in order to capture anyone's attention today you have to hit them right between the eyes with something that will make them sit up and take notice. Something "they" will remember. With these climactic scenes, I know everyone has that chance.

PART ONE:
Two Women

SCENE 1 — Nancy and Ariel
Age Level 23-38

SCENE OPENS: NANCY and ARIEL are sisters. NANCY is sitting on her sofa, reading the paper. The bell rings and NANCY answers door.

NANCY: What do you want?

ARIEL: I've come to talk to you.

NANCY: I'm busy. I don't have time for you.

ARIEL: *(Pushing past her)* **Make the time then.**

NANCY: Hey, I didn't invite you in.

ARIEL: Oh, that's right. I need to be male to be invited.

NANCY: Look — don't condemn me for doing exactly what you yourself would like to do — if you had half my guts and a third of my looks.

ARIEL: Close the door Nancy. This will be private. Unlike your sleeping habits.

NANCY: Get to the point Ariel. Why are you here?

ARIEL: I want you to sign these papers.

NANCY: *(Reading them. Laughs)* **You can't be serious. These papers are for custody of Johnny.**

ARIEL: I'm gratified to find that you can still read *and* comprehend.

NANCY: How can you possibly expect me to sign over my own son. To you?

ARIEL: Don't pretend any mother love with me Nancy. I know how you're just using Johnny to extract payments from at least three prominent businessmen, one congressman and God knows who else, claiming to each — that he's their son.

NANCY: How do you know that? Have you had me followed? Or bugged my phone?

ARIEL: It wasn't as devious as you might think. In fact, it was rather easy. Kind of like you.

1   NANCY: Even if you do know — what makes you think that I
2   would willingly hand over my own son? He's my only
3   source of income . . . and I love him.
4   ARIEL: Source of income. What an interesting name for your,
5   let me quote you, *(Reads from letter)* **"Precious bundle of**
6   **Joy".** You must have confused the word precious with
7   priceless.
8   NANCY: Let me see that! *(Grabs papers.)* How did you get this?
9   You know Ariel, stealing mail is a federal offense.
10   ARIEL: It was *given* to me. So now I have all the documentation
11   I need to get you to release Johnny into my custody.
12   NANCY: *(Scornfully)* No you don't. You just have a few pieces
13   of paper, that's all. *(Throws them back to her.)*
14   ARIEL: Incriminating papers. Your plan to marry Jasper
15   Ellington would blow skyhigh if he knew what you were
16   really like. I'll show these to him unless you sign.
17   NANCY: No you won't. You're pathetic. You just want Johnny
18   because you're sterile. Barren as a desert. Well, you're
19   not going to get my Johnny so you can feel like a real
20   woman again. No way.
21   ARIEL: Being sterile doesn't make me less of a woman. This
22   isn't a warning, Nancy. Jasper gets this package as my
23   pre-nuptial wedding gift unless you cooperate.
24   NANCY: Even *you* couldn't be that low. You'd be stealing my
25   baby.
26   ARIEL: With the many things you've stolen from me — we
27   can call this even Stephen.
28   NANCY: You're out of your mind. I won't do it.
29   ARIEL: Suit yourself. *(Starts to go.)*
30   NANCY: Wait! But . . . how will I manage?
31   ARIEL: You'll think of something. You always do. Why don't
32   you try talking Jasper into an early marriage. Elope.
33   That's always romantic and stupid. Just up your alley.
34   NANCY: You've got to give me some time. I can't think straight.
35   *(Sits)*

1   ARIEL: *(Goes to her.)* **Come on Nancy, play it smart for once.**
2   **Sign the damn thing and get it over with.**
3   NANCY: **Can't we sit down and ...**
4   ARIEL: **Forget it! Either I leave with those papers signed —**
5   **or Jasper gets a surprise visit.**
6   NANCY: **Ariel — I may not be the best mother in the world,**
7   **but I really do love Johnny. And if you ...**
8   ARIEL: **Cut it out! Sign or don't sign, but please — save the**
9   **hearts and flowers for Valentines Day.**
10   NANCY: *(Beat)* **Give me the damn thing!** *(Signs)* **There! Now I**
11   **really do feel sorry for little Johnny. I've signed away his**
12   **life into eighteen years of pure Hell.**
13   ARIEL: *(Walks to door.)* **Think of the consolation. If you died**
14   **early — you'd be able to visit.**
15   *(ARIEL exits.)*
16
17
18
19
20
21
22
23
24
25
26
27
28
29
30
31
32
33
34
35

SCENE 2 — Constance and Patty
Age Level 22-38
3

4   ***SCENE OPENS:***   CONSTANCE and PATTY are best friends. Bell
5   rings and CONSTANCE runs to answer it.

6

7   **CONSTANCE:**   **Finally!** *(Takes the groceries.)* **What took you so**
8   **long? You made me a nervous wreck.** *(Starts bringing the*
9   *bundles into the other room.)*
10 **PATTY: I'm fine. Just a little shaken up but nothing serious.**
11 **CONSTANCE: Shaken up? What are you talking about?**
12 **PATTY: I had an accident.**
13 **CONSTANCE: Accident?!** *(Looking in the bag)* **I hope the eggs**
14   **didn't break.**
15 **PATTY: They're in better shape than my car. I bumped the**
16   **side fender and banged my head. It's a toss up whether**
17   **my car suffered more damage or my head.**
18 **CONSTANCE: I hope you have insurance. You just got that**
19   **car.** *(Goes to kitchen.)*
20 **PATTY: Of course, I do.** *(Sits down on couch.)* **Got any ice? I**
21   **have a wicked headache.**
22 **CONSTANCE:**   *(From Offstage)* **Oh no, Patty. The party's**
23   **tonight. You know, I heard that if you ignore pain, it**
24   **usually goes away by itself.**
25 **PATTY: Ice Connie. And aspirin.** *(Droops down onto the couch,*
26   *arm covering face.)* **Quickly!**
27 **CONSTANCE: You're not planning on lying down, are you?**
28   *(Comes out from the kitchen.)* **There are a million and one**
29   **things that still need to be done.**
30 **PATTY: Connie, my head is splitting. For all I know, I may**
31   **have a concussion.**
32 **CONSTANCE: Can't you concuss — after the party?**
33 **PATTY: Nice of you to be so concerned.**
34 **CONSTANCE: I am concerned. About you *and* the party.**
35 **PATTY: Don't make me feel guilty, OK?** *(Sits up.)* **Your party**

1	preparations are all done . . .
2	CONSTANCE: Except the food. Who's going to devil the eggs?
3	And you do such a beautiful job with the radish rosettes.
4	PATTY: The party can do without the rosettes. Besides, you
5	have caterers coming. Maybe one of them knows how to
6	do it.
7	CONSTANCE: I was counting on you. This party is important
8	to me. At least stay and help me greet the guests. That's
9	the least you could do.
10	PATTY: I can't. The way my head feels, I doubt if I will be able
11	to see, let alone speak this evening.
12	CONSTANCE: All right, fine. Take off. Leave me in my most
13	desperate hour. I'm sure I'll manage to survive somehow.
14	PATTY: Thanks. I knew you would understand. *(Starts to leave.)*
15	CONSTANCE: Patty. *(Goes to her.)* Now that you mention it,
16	you don't look well. Maybe you ought to stay here for a
17	little while, just to make sure you don't go into convulsions
18	or something.
19	PATTY: Convulsions?!
20	CONSTANCE: Yes. I read that somewhere. Head injuries
21	sometimes cause the victim to go into convulsions.
22	PATTY: I'm just a little tired. But I do have a blinding headache.
23	CONSTANCE: See? For safety's sake, why don't you go
24	upstairs and rest. I'll wake you up in an hour or so and
25	then you can see how you feel.
26	PATTY: I'll probably feel rotten. I should really be in my own
27	bed the whole evening. *(Turns to go.)*
28	CONSTANCE: No, stay! Who knows, maybe you'll feel well
29	enough to join the party.
30	PATTY: Connie!
31	CONSTANCE: You never can tell. Besides, I promise if you
32	still want to go home, I'll personally drive you and tuck
33	you in.
34	PATTY: I'm too sick to argue with you. I'm going home.
35	CONSTANCE: Come here. *(Goes to her and looks in her eyes.)*

1   Just as I thought. They're dilated. Go on upstairs and
2   I'll bring the ice and aspirin. *(As PATTY hesitates)* **Go on.**
3   **I'll be up in a minute.**
4 **PATTY:**   You promise you'll drive me home later — without
5   any hassles?
6 **CONSTANCE:**   Cross my heart.
7 **PATTY:**   You don't have one.
8 **CONSTANCE:**   You're becoming cranky. A sure sign you need
9   to lie down. Now scoot. I have a zillion things to finish up.
10 **PATTY:**   Maybe you're right. *(Turns at door.)* **Thanks Con.**
11   **Sorry about your party.** *(PATTY exits.)*
12 **CONSTANCE:**   Oh . . . I'll survive. *(Goes to phone and starts to*
13   *dial.)*
14
15
16
17
18
19
20
21
22
23
24
25
26
27
28
29
30
31
32
33
34
35

SCENE 3 — Terry and Ingrid
Age Level 20-45

SCENE OPENS: TERRY and INGRID are having a drink in TERRY's apartment. They are sisters, INGRID being the elder. They are in the living room with a kitchen to the side.

TERRY: **Down with men!**

INGRID: **You can't live with 'em and ya can't live without 'em.**

TERRY: **You're drunk!**

INGRID: **I most certainly am not.**

TERRY: **Yes you are. Whenever you start spouting clichés, I know you're well on your way to becoming pickled.**

INGRID: **I've only had three, and I can hold at least five. Six on a good day.**

TERRY: **Let's have some coffee.**

INGRID: **Coffee sounds great.**

TERRY: *(Trys to get up, but doesn't have the strength.)* **If I can pry myself off the couch, I'll make us some. You know, you're the greatest sister in the world.**

INGRID: **You're prejudiced.**

TERRY: **No I'm not. You're probably the greatest sister in the universe.**

INGRID: **Uh, oh. You're becoming sentimental. Maybe *I* better make the coffee.** *(Gets up and goes to kitchen which is part of living room.)*

TERRY: *(While INGRID is making coffee)* **Ingrid, do you hate Jeffrey? I mean *really* hate him.**

INGRID: **Sometimes. Most times. I think I hate the image of myself he left me with. Leaving me for another woman . . . another younger woman, makes a person feel, disposable. Like an old shoe.**

TERRY: **Well, I hate him. I hate him for what he's done to you.**

INGRID: **I'll live. Let's get off this depressing topic and talk about something else.**

1   TERRY: I hear there's this great movie playing down at the
2   Melrose . . . never mind, you wouldn't like it.
3   INGRID: *(Comes out.)* Why not? I love movies. We'll buy a large
4   box of junior mints and indulge our fantasies. What's it
5   about?
6   TERRY: Love. *(Pause)* Why does the movie world make love
7   and romance look so simple, when in reality it's the
8   hardest thing to achieve. It seems so easy when it's in
9   Technicolor℠.
10 INGRID: I know what you mean. Even the music fits. *(She*
11   *smiles to self.)*
12 TERRY: What's so funny?
13 INGRID: That's one of the things that Jeffrey said we didn't
14   have. "The music's gone, Ingrid. I don't hear anything
15   when I look at you."
16 TERRY: Jeez, I'm so mad. I always looked to you and Jeff as
17   the perfect couple. You got along so well. I remember you
18   always seemed to have such fun together. You were
19   always laughing.
20 INGRID: Maybe instead of laughing with me, Jeff was
21   laughing at me. I don't know.
22 TERRY: Well, I know I can't trust men anymore.
23 INGRID: Nonsense. You'll meet someone special, you'll fall in
24   love and you'll do the same things that everyone else does.
25 TERRY: No I won't. *(Beat)* When you told me what happened,
26   do you know how I felt? Like a cold icy hand passed over
27   my heart.
28 INGRID: Oh baby, I didn't mean to put you through that.
29   When I told you how I felt, those feelings needed to come
30   out so they wouldn't poison me. But they aren't a part of
31   me now.
32 TERRY: But they're a part of me. I'm afraid.
33 INGRID: Of what?
34 TERRY: I don't want reality to catch me unawares like it
35   caught you. I don't want to find myself the brunt of parlor

1   jokes and snide remarks said behind raised hands.
2   INGRID: Terry, I ...
3   TERRY: Or worse — sympathy and pity murmured out of the
4   mouths of "friends" while they cross your name off the
5   desirable guest list.
6   INGRID: Terry, this isn't like you. Where's your cheerful
7   spirit and optimistic outlook? Come on kiddo, you're
8   depressing me.
9   TERRY: Sorry. Don't mind me — just the alcohol talking.
10   Now, where's that coffee? *(Goes towards kitchen. INGRID*
11   *has closeout.)*
12
13
14
15
16
17
18
19
20
21
22
23
24
25
26
27
28
29
30
31
32
33
34
35

SCENE 4 — Lauren and Nancy
Age Level 20-30

1
2
3
4   ***SCENE OPENS:*** LAUREN is pacing back and forth looking at the
5   phone. NANCY is reading the paper.
6
7   **LAUREN:** Men! They are so . . . unreliable.
8   **NANCY:** I've heard you call them many things. But unreliable
9   is a new one.
10 **LAUREN:** But that word describes them perfectly. Unreliable.
11   Right down to their toes.
12 **NANCY:** What happened now?
13 **LAUREN:** Nothing. That's just the point.
14 **NANCY:** Didn't Jason call you like he said he would?
15 **LAUREN:** No he did not. He also said he would take me to
16   dinner, but look at the time. Seven-thirty and he hasn't
17   called to see *where* I want to go.
18 **NANCY:** Don't worry, he'll call. He always does.
19 **LAUREN:** I don't care anymore. But he should find out what I
20   want to do *earlier.* Suppose I decide I don't want to go to
21   dinner after all?
22 **NANCY:** Then he'll probably grab a hamburger by himself,
23   before he comes over.
24 **LAUREN:** Suppose I want to do something else right away?
25   Something totally different.
26 **NANCY:** Then you'll tell him what you want to do — on the
27   phone. When he calls.
28 **LAUREN:** But . . .
29 **NANCY:** But nothing. You're making trouble were there
30   shouldn't be any. *(Puts down paper.)* Why do you like to do that?
31 **LAUREN:** I don't like to do that.
32 **NANCY:** Yes you do. You do it every time you get bored with a
33   relationship. People are not toys, Lauren.
34 **LAUREN:** I never said they were.
35 **NANCY:** Right. *(Picks paper back up.)*

1	LAUREN: You sound upset. Did I say something to upset
2	you?
3	NANCY: No. *(Puts paper aside.)* You just don't seem to have
4	much regard for people and their feelings, that's all.
5	LAUREN: That's not true. *(Beat)* You know, when I broke up
6	with Rob — you told me you wouldn't hold that against
7	me.
8	NANCY: I didn't and I'm not.
9	LAUREN: Oh yes you are. If your brother means more to you
10	than our friendship, then maybe you ought to room with
11	someone else.
12	NANCY: What? *(Realization)* Wait a minute. We've been
13	roommates for too long for you to think you can pull a
14	fast one over on me like that!
15	LAUREN: What fast one?
16	NANCY: The famous Lauren "Fast Shuffle". You're trying to
17	get me out of this apartment, aren't you?
18	LAUREN: I don't know what you're talking about.
19	NANCY: Don't lie. I happen to know you've been looking for
20	someone to pay a little more of the rent. I was just
21	wondering when you were going to tell me.
22	LAUREN: I've been doing no such thing. I mentioned —
23	mentioned — that it would be nice to have a little more
24	cash at the end of the month, that's all.
25	NANCY: We signed this lease together. That means fifty-fifty,
26	so get used to the fact that the "little extra cash" is going
27	to have to come from another source. Not my pocket — and
28	not by me moving out. *(NANCY exits.)*
29	LAUREN: *(To self)* Isn't she touchy today.
30	
31	
32	
33	
34	
35	

SCENE 5 — Rose and Susan

Age Level 20-45

SCENE OPENS: ROSE and SUSAN are sisters. ROSE is older and SUSAN suffers from tuberculosis. ROSE enters and sees SUSAN preparing the vegetables at the dining table.

ROSE: Well, aren't we the domestic one. What happened? Get bored sitting around all day, doing nothing?

SUSAN: Someone's got to do the cooking or we'd all eat at midnight. Besides, I felt better today.

ROSE: Praise the Lord, the queen felt better today.

SUSAN: Lay off Rose. I'm not into bickering right now.

ROSE: Neither am I. I just get a little peeved when I come home from working my butt off and see you looking so fresh and rosy. How come if you're sick, you can look so energetic when you want to?

SUSAN: It has nothing to do with, when I want to. You know that.

ROSE: All I know is, I usually get stuck carrying most of the load around here. Tell me something. What did you do most of the day?

SUSAN: What difference does it make?

ROSE: Uh, huh. Just what I thought. Instead of convalescing so that maybe you could *help* with the work around here, you were off painting, weren't you?

SUSAN: Yes I was painting. Painting makes me feel good. Painting makes me forget my lungs once in a while. Is that so bad?

ROSE: You're damn right it's bad. You're weakening yourself when you do that. And if you weaken anymore — you could be dead.

SUSAN: Unfortunately for me — *(Turns back to her vegetables)* I don't think that's going to be for a while.

ROSE: Always thinking of yourself. If you up and die, all

1	these years we've carried you will be for nothing. Instead
2	of having an extra hand to help with the work, there'll
3	be one less.
4	SUSAN: You're so practical Rose. I had no idea you were so
5	business oriented.
6	ROSE: I know what's right. Painting is the same as dreaming.
7	Useless and stupid.
8	SUSAN: Thanks. All I know is, I feel rejuvenated when I paint.
9	I feel happy. *(Starts to breathe deeply.)*
10	ROSE: Rejuvenated, hell! I think you're lazy. I think you're
11	playing this family for all you can get.
12	SUSAN: You know that's not true! *(Breathing gets harder.)*
13	Damn, damn! You always manage to get to me Rose, don't
14	you? You always know just what to say. *(She leans over*
15	*table and starts wheezing.)*
16	ROSE: *(Beat)* Don't gasp over my vegetables girl. You might
17	contaminate them. *(She exits.)*
18	
19	
20	
21	
22	
23	
24	
25	
26	
27	
28	
29	
30	
31	
32	
33	
34	
35	

SCENE 6 — Mindy and Annette
Age Level 22-32

SCENE OPENS: MINDY and ANNETTE are sisters. MINDY has an apartment in the city, ANNETTE lives in Connecticut. The bell rings in MINDY's house and she answers it.

MINDY: Nettie!

ANNETTE: Surprise!

MINDY: What are you doing here? This is Tuesday, isn't it?

ANNETTE: *(Enters)* Yes it's Tuesday. But I thought I'd visit you anyway.

MINDY: Uh, oh. It's not your usual day to venture into the big bad city, so what's up?

ANNETTE: Nothing's up. I thought I would come in and see my sister. I'm allowed, aren't I? *(Sits)*

MINDY: Yes you're allowed. Except for the fact that you usually want something from me when the visit comes out of the blue like this.

ANNETTE: Don't be so suspicious. Have you had lunch yet?

MINDY: No. *(Beat)* Sorry, I didn't mean to . . .

ANNETTE: You're forgiven.

MINDY: This is a first. You're actually visiting me. How nice.

ANNETTE: Yes nice. Do you have anything in your refrigerator? Or should I scoot down to the deli? 'Course I'd probably have to know Spanish, just to order something.

MINDY: Don't start. José knows English as well as Spanish. He's just a little unsure using it.

ANNETTE: Oh, that's right. He's part of the New York bi-lingual culture that you enjoy so much.

MINDY: *(Changing subject)* So. How's Ken?

ANNETTE: Fine. Mom and Dad are fine too. They're looking forward to next week.

MINDY: Next week? They don't go to Florida till next month.

ANNETTE: I know, but next week is important to them. It's

1	important to *all* of us. Isn't it?
2	MINDY: Is it? *(Beat)* **Oh Christ! Their anniversary.** *(Seeing*
3	*ANNETTE's expectant face.)* **No way — get that gleam right**
4	**out of your eyes. I am not going to be roped into another**
5	**one of your extravaganzas.**
6	ANNETTE: It's not an extravaganza. And what do you mean
7	roped?
8	MINDY: R-O-P-E-D. As in, tied up and practically strangled.
9	ANNETTE: Mindy, that's unfair. I've never asked you to do
10	anything you didn't end up enjoying.
11	MINDY: Oh, no? Who was "Quacky The Clown" at Nancy's
12	third birthday? I still have laryngitis from screaming "let
13	me go" and "give that back". Trust me Annette, I did not
14	enjoy myself.
15	ANNETTE: This is different. It's for Mom and Dad and they'll
16	be so disappointed if you aren't there to help out.
17	MINDY: Too bad. I hated the last party you planned because
18	I got stuck doing everything.
19	ANNETTE: You did not. *I* mailed out all the invitations.
20	MINDY: That's right you *mailed* them. After I wrote each and
21	every one out by "hand" for that special touch you
22	thought they needed.
23	ANNETTE: Someone has to supervise. I did my share. I
24	handled all the food preparations.
25	MINDY: Calling up the caterers is not my idea of handling all
26	the food. In fact, I walked around half the night passing
27	out the hors d'oeuvres when one of the maids went home
28	early.
29	ANNETTE: And I appreciated it. Everyone had to do their part.
30	MINDY: Is that so? I don't think my part should have been
31	walking around with a maid's uniform on, asking people
32	if they wanted more pigs-in-the-blanket or caviar quiche!
33	ANNETTE: But you looked so cute in that outfit. Everyone
34	thought so.
35	MINDY: Annette, read my lips. I'm not helping out this year.

1   **If you want to throw a party, then throw one. Only do it**

2   **without me.**

3 **ANNETTE:**   **OK.** *(Gathers her things. Said sweetly)* **I don't know**

4   **why I should be surprised. You never think of anyone**

5   **else but yourself.**

6 **MINDY:**   **It's not going to work this time.**

7 **ANNETTE:**   **I suppose you think I'm trying to manipulate you.**

8   **In all seriousness Mindy, you're much too selfish to fall**

9   **for that. I'll see you at the party . . . that is, if there is one.**

10 *(Exits)*

11

12

13

14

15

16

17

18

19

20

21

22

23

24

25

26

27

28

29

30

31

32

33

34

35

SCENE 7 — Margaret and Valerie
Age Level 22-52

SCENE OPENS: MARGARET is VALERIE's mother. The house is
   dark and VALERIE is sitting alone on a chair by the window.
   MARGARET enters and passing through, sees her.

MARGARET: Valerie? What are you doing here in the dark?
   Are you all right?

VALERIE: I'm fine.

MARGARET: Why are you sitting all alone? It's depressing.
   Kids today are so morbid, *(Starts toward the kitchen)* let me
   fix you some tea.

VALERIE: I don't want any tea. I want to be alone and think.

MARGARET: Well, you don't need to think in the dark. *(Turns
   on light.)* I hate the dark. It reminds me of death.

VALERIE: That's funny. I do feel a little dead right now.

MARGARET: Sweetheart, what's the matter? *(Pats hand)* Oh,
   feel your hands. They're like ice. Let me get you a blanket.

VALERIE: I don't need a blanket. *(Stares at her.)*

MARGARET: Stop looking at me like that. You really frighten
   me when you get so intense. What is it?

VALERIE: I've just discovered something so . . . ludicrous
   that I can hardly believe it.

MARGARET: What? *(She is silent.)* Valerie, I know it's difficult
   for you to share your feelings with your mother — but I'm
   always open to anything that might be troubling you. Tell
   me what it is.

VALERIE: *(Beat)* It's about James.

MARGARET: *(Stands abruptly.)* I don't want to hear it. Anything
   that has to do with that low life, is not worth repeating.
   (Starts to go.)

VALERIE: Mother! *(Stands)* Until now, I never understood
   what you had against my dating James. I never understood
   why you hated him so much.

1   MARGARET: I don't hate him. The only reason I didn't want
2   you dating him is because I think he's inferior and will
3   amount to no good. Why? Has someone said something
4   to the contrary?
5   VALERIE: Oh, yes. *(Walks to her.)* Someone has said a lot to the
6   contrary.
7   MARGARET: They're a filthy liar.
8   VALERIE: Hardly. It was Reverend Johnson.
9   MARGARET: Reverend . . . my God. What has he done? *(Sits)*
10   VALERIE: Only told me the truth. The truth that should
11   have come out of your mouth. *(Starts to pace.)* Why mother?
12   Why didn't you tell me yourself?
13   MARGARET: *(Grabbing at straws.)* I . . . I'm not sure I know
14   what you're talking about.
15   VALERIE: *(Angry)* Don't continue the lie. I know all about
16   James.
17   MARGARET: Damn him. Damn him straight to Hell! Why did
18   that busybody have to tell you? It was none of his
19   business.
20   VALERIE: It became his business. He saw James and me
21   down at City Hall trying to get a marriage license.
22   MARGARET: A what? You never told me you were . . .
23   VALERIE: And I wasn't planning on telling you either. Not
24   until James and I had become man and wife. *(Laughs)* I
25   thought you would relent, once we had . . .
26   MARGARET: How much of the story did the Reverend tell
27   James?
28   VALERIE: None. He told me in private. Then I left.
29   MARGARET: Thank God!
30   VALERIE: Thank God? I have to tell James something! For
31   all he knows, I just got cold feet and ran out on him.
32   MARGARET: He'll get over it. *(Gets up and goes to her.)* Valerie,
33   think logically. You certainly don't plan on telling him
34   the truth, do you?
35   VALERIE: Why not? He deserves an explanation.

1   MARGARET: Then fabricate one. If this story should get out,
2   I'll be ruined . . . we'll be ruined.
3   VALERIE: I don't care.
4   MARGARET: Admirable of you. But . . . how do you think
5   James will feel? — Poor boy.
6   VALERIE: *(Beat)* **Repulsed.**
7   MARGARET: Exactly! So, why put him through that? Listen
8   to me. If you make him think you don't love him and
9   never did, he won't pressure you for reasons.
10   VALERIE: *(Quietly)* **He knows how much I love him.**
11   MARGARET: Then it will be your duty to make him see that
12   you don't. Valerie. *(Grabs her by the shoulders and she pulls*
13   *away.)* **Look at me! The truth will only make him hate**
14   you. It will be far crueler to let him know you love him
15   and yet never tell him the reason you can't be married.
16   VALERIE: God. What am I going to do?
17   MARGARET: Oh, honey. *(Takes her arms.)* I'm sorry. I really am.
18   VALERIE: Don't touch me. And don't you *dare* try to pretend
19   that you *feel* anything. You only regret that I know about
20   you.
21   MARGARET: That's not it at all. Of course I feel . . .
22   VALERIE: No you don't. You never feel. You never have.
23   *(Starts to leave.)*
24   MARGARET: You have every right to be upset . . . but before
25   you go, there's something I need to know. How far have
26   you and James gone in . . . in . . .
27   VALERIE: You mean did I sleep with him Mother? Sleep
28   with my own *brother?* That's something you'll never
29   know. Something you can speculate about when you go
30   to church. Something you'll find out about in Hell!
31   *(VALERIE exits.)*
32
33
34
35

SCENE 8 — Mona and Jasmin

Age Level 30-40

SCENE OPENS: MONA and JASMIN used to be friends in high school. MONA has found JASMIN after all these years to offer her a business opportunity. They walk into the living room, MONA's delivery is light till end.

MONA: A model? I didn't go through all the trouble to find you to have you deny what you are. You're a call girl, pure and simple, so let's get down to negotiations.

JASMIN: I *am* a model. I only go out with men like that when I get hungry. That's something I don't think you know anything about, do you?

MONA: Don't try to make me feel guilty because you sell your body to make ends meet. That's your choice. Funny, but it's been your choice to use your body any and every way you could, ever since we were kids.

JASMIN: You're damn right! Why shouldn't I use something that God gave me. It's been a curse for so long, why not turn it into an asset?

MONA: Why? Because you're beginning to look tired around the edges. But that's something else you'll probably lie about to yourself till it's too late.

JASMIN: Tired around the edges? *(Goes to mirror.)* What a nasty thing to say.

MONA: Nasty, but truthful. Look, I came over here to give you some business, not flatter you. Let's talk money. How much?

JASMIN: I ought to slap your face.

MONA: But you won't. Do you want to drop the facade for just a little bit, or . . . do you want to forget the whole thing? *(Starts to gather up her things.)*

JASMIN: *(Beat)* **What exactly are we talking about here? Who is it and for how long?**

1	MONA: At last. All right, his name's Mark Desmond and he'll
2	be in town for two days . . . and nights.
3	JASMIN: Two days? I'm not sure I can give up that much
4	time. I . . . I have things to do.
5	MONA: Oh, come on, Jasmin. It's just two days out of your
6	life. That's not much to ask.
7	JASMIN: Why is this so important to you?
8	MONA: Let's just say, he's a very, very good client.
9	JASMIN: What are his interests?
10	MONA: Money.
11	JASMIN: Well, now that does sound interesting. Anything
12	else?
13	MONA: Why don't you just find out. You two might have lots
14	in common. Wouldn't it be more fun to find out for
15	yourself? Now, *(Takes out checkbook)* how much?
16	JASMIN: Don't rush me, I'm thinking. Two thousand dollars
17	plus expenses, for the two . . . days. Nonrefundable.
18	MONA: A package deal. Very nice. What expenses are we
19	talking about?
20	JASMIN: Cleaning bills for any gowns I might use. Flowers
21	for the apartment. I get a facial before and after, a
22	massage and . . . oh yes, a check-up.
23	MONA: Very business-like. Very professional. *(She looks her*
24	*up and down.)*
25	JASMIN: Don't look at me like that. You're no better than I am.
26	MONA: No better than you? A common whore? Really, Jasmin.
27	*(Gathers her coat leaving check on the coffee table.)*
28	JASMIN: Whore?! Why you bitch! If I'm a whore then you're
29	a pimp.
30	MONA: Maybe. But at least I don't have to get a check-up
31	after I'm done.
32	JASMIN: Get out of here! And you can forget our little deal.
33	I don't need the money that badly. *(Gets check and rips it up.)*
34	MONA: Gee, Mark will be so disappointed. He's been looking
35	forward to seeing you again.

1   JASMIN: Seeing me again? I don't know any Mark Desmond.

2   MONA: Oh, I think you do. He used to call himself Nick
3   Holister.

4   JASMIN: Nick?! You were going to set me up with Nick?
5   How could you do that to me?

6   MONA: It was easy. You set yourself up. Now, I'm going to
7   call ol' Nick and tell him I've finally found you and that
8   you're dying to see him.

9   JASMIN: No! *(Panicked)* No, please don't do that. I don't want
10   to see him.

11 MONA: Don't beg. I never did like to see you beg. You said
12   yes, so that's the deal. Take it or leave it. When I tell Nick
13   where you are he's going to come here anyway. You might
14   as well get paid for it. You know how . . . difficult it is to
15   say no to Nick.

16 JASMIN: Why would you do this? Why do you hate me this
17   much?

18 MONA: You used to go out of your way to steal whatever I
19   had or wanted. I call this, the Payoff.

20 JASMIN: I was a stupid kid then. I always thought I would
21   be happy if I had what you had. You seemed so . . .
22   content.

23 MONA: I wasn't. You made me miserable. Now it's my turn.

24 JASMIN: You can go to Hell! I won't be here. I'll go someplace
25   else. Another city. Another town.

26 MONA: You won't be that hard to find, considering your
27   chosen profession. And if we wait long enough, we can
28   just cruise the red light district.

29 JASMIN: *(Advancing towards her)* And now I think I really will
30   slap your face.

31 MONA: *(At the door)* Look at you now. My, how the mighty
32   have fallen. See you 'round, former "Beauty Queen". Let's
33   hope the pages in our yearbook hold up better than you
34   will.

35   *(MONA exits.)*

– 24 –

SCENE 9 — Clara and Jane
Age Level 15-18

SCENE OPENS: JANE is standing with a school cafeteria tray in
       hand. CLARA is sitting eating lunch. JANE looks surreptitiously
       around as CLARA speaks.

CLARA: Gossip?! Is it meaty?

JANE: The meatiest!

CLARA: Don't stand there like a stick. Sit down and tell me.

JANE: OK. *(Sits)* But I can't divulge names.

CLARA: Jane, what's gossip without names? A bird without
       feathers. A sock without a shoe.

JANE: If I tell — it could mean a head without a body.

CLARA: Don't be stupid. Besides, who would know?

JANE: I think he saw me when I ducked down. And I don't
       want anyone to know *I* told.

CLARA: He who? *(At her look)* OK, OK.

JANE: Well — a certain male party was seen taking a certain
       female party to Main Street yesterday.

CLARA: And?

JANE: And the certain male party dropped her off in front
       of — Dr. Zallinger's.

CLARA: The abortionist?!

JANE: You got it.

CLARA: Who?!

JANE: Ask me no questions and I'll tell you no lies.

CLARA: Jane!

JANE: My lips are sealed. *(Beat)* Come on Clara, play detective.
       (The following exchange is done very quickly.)

CLARA: Do I know this person?

JANE: Yes.

CLARA: Is she tall?

JANE: No.

CLARA: Short?

1   JANE: Yes.
2   CLARA: Blonde?
3   JANE: Ummmm ...
4   CLARA: Brunette.
5   JANE: Ahhhh ...
6   CLARA: ... with blonde highlights!
7   JANE: Yes!
8   CLARA: Brown eyes.
9   JANE: Yes!
10   CLARA: Great waist but big legs.
11   JANE: Yes!
12   CLARA: Mandy!
13   JANE: Yes! Ooops. *(Covers mouth.)* I didn't tell, you guessed.
14   CLARA: You're kidding?! Mandy? That little Miss Goody-two-
15   shoes?
16   JANE: Surprised me too. Course — she could have just been
17   getting a check-up ... or meeting someone.
18   CLARA: Right. *(Beat. Both laugh)* I bet. So, who's the guy?
19   Steve?
20   JANE: Noooo.
21   CLARA: Greg? *(JANE shakes head at all names.)* Martin?
22   Jimmy? Bobby? Well, who then? There isn't anybody else
23   left.
24   JANE: Maybe there is and maybe there isn't.
25   CLARA: *(Beat)* Scott?
26   JANE: I wouldn't have breathed a word except I knew you'd
27   want to be the first to know.
28   CLARA: I have no dibs on him. Scott and I broke up last
29   month. *(Beat)* Why, that little slut. All this time pretending
30   she was so pure ...
31   JANE: And with Scott. No wonder you two were having
32   problems.
33   CLARA: She had nothing to do with our problems. He's a
34   jerk and I woke up one morning, realized it and told him
35   to take a hike, that's all.

1 JANE: Oh. I thought . . .

2 CLARA: Don't think. That's your trouble Jane, you try doing
3   things you're not good at.

4 JANE: Hey! Don't get mad at me. I didn't steal Scott away
5   from you.

6 CLARA: Neither did Mandy!

7 JANE: OK, calm down. *(Beat)* What are you gonna do?

8 CLARA: Find out the truth — then post the doctor bills on
9   all the school hallways, corridors, bathroom stalls,
10   lockers . . .

11 JANE: That's absolutely diabolical. *(Beat)* It's also confidential.
12   How'll you get a copy?

13 CLARA: Jane my girl — haven't you ever heard of breaking
14   and entering? And Dr. Zallinger's office will be easy, he's
15   out a lot.

16 JANE: What?! No way. My folks would kill me.

17 CLARA: Not if they don't find out. Don't you think we should
18   be good little citizens and let her parents know about
19   her abortion?

20 JANE: Suppose it isn't true?

21 CLARA: Oh, it's true all right! I'd bet on it. *(At JANE's reluctance)*
22   Come on — we won't get caught.

23 JANE: Suppose we don't find anything incriminating?

24 CLARA: We will. I'll find something, one way or another.

25   *(Fade out)*

26

27

28

29

30

31

32

33

34

35

SCENE 10 — Laura and Barbara
Age Level 18-28

SCENE OPENS: LAURA rings bell at BARBARA's house. BARBARA opens door. LAURA is dressed in coat, carrying gloves.

LAURA: *(Pushing past her)* **Is Joe here?**

BARBARA: **No. Should he be?**

LAURA: **You tell me.**

BARBARA: **I'd have a better chance of answering that if you tell me what you want.**

LAURA: **Judy told me she'd seen you and Joe down at Lookout Point. Is it true?**

BARBARA: *(Beat)* **Yes.** *(Turns away.)* **But it's not what you think.**

LAURA: **And what *do* I think Barbara?** *(Pulling her around)*

BARBARA: **I didn't break my promise, if that's what you mean. Joe just needed to talk, that's all.**

LAURA: **People don't *talk* down at Lookout Point.**

BARBARA: **Joe wanted somewhere private. I certainly didn't expect big mouth Judy to be there.**

LAURA: **She happens to be my friend.**

BARBARA: **Friends mind their own business.**

LAURA: **Joe happens to *be* my business. So what were you doing with him last night? In fact, what were you doing with him Tuesday night?**

BARBARA: *(Beat)* **You should talk to Joe about this, Laura. Not me.**

LAURA: **So you admit it.**

BARBARA: **I admit I met him — but at his insistence and it has nothing to do with us as a couple. That's been over and done with a long time ago.**

LAURA: **So you say.** *(Pause)* **What's going on?**

BARBARA: **Ask Joe!**

LAURA: **I have.** *(Beat)* **He's stopped taking my calls.**

1   BARBARA: I'm sorry, Laura. But I can't help you.
2   LAURA: You've got to. I can't stand it anymore. He won't talk
3   to me. See me. *(She sits.)* I'm going crazy.
4   BARBARA: Then trust him enough to let you know in his own
5   time.
6   LAURA: I can't. *(Beat)* It's serious, isn't it?
7   BARBARA: He doesn't want to involve you right now.
8   LAURA: A little late for that. I'm already involved.
9   BARBARA: Not in this and you need to keep it that way.
10   Trust me, Laura. *(Takes pity on her.)* All I'll tell you is it's
11   dangerous — and you're well out of it. *(LAURA gets up and*
12   *starts to leave.)* Where are you going?
13   LAURA: *(Slowly putting on gloves)* To have an overdue chat
14   with Chambers.
15   BARBARA: Chambers?!
16   LAURA: 'Course I should have figured it out before this.
17   BARBARA: *(Nervous)* What are you talking about?
18   LAURA: That whenever something goes wrong in my life,
19   Chambers usually figures in it. Besides danger and
20   Chambers go hand in hand. *(Starts to go.)* Thanks for the
21   tip.
22   BARBARA: *(Pulling her back)* Listen to me, Laura. That man
23   is the last person you should see right now.
24   LAURA: Exactly why I'm going. He may be many things, but
25   at least he'll tell me what's going on. *(Pausing at door)* Who
26   am I kidding? He's probably behind it. *(Exits)*
27   BARBARA: *(Frightened. To self)* Me and my big mouth.
28
29
30
31
32
33
34
35

1	# SCENE 11 — Stacy and Bonnie
2	*Age Level 20-45*
3	

SCENE OPENS: STACY and BONNIE are sisters. STACY rings BONNIE's bell. BONNIE is dramatically draped on sofa, slightly rumpled, but doesn't answer. STACY lets herself in and stops, seeing BONNIE.

STACY: I knew it! *(Slams door.)* Bonnie, we had a date today. Where were you?

BONNIE: *(Sitting up)* I got tied up at the beauty parlor and decided it wasn't worth the trouble. So I came home.

STACY: And didn't call to cancel? Typical!

BONNIE: Sorry, Stacy.

STACY: I checked Henrietta's and you weren't scheduled and you didn't show. So where were you really?

BONNIE: Henrietta's? Oh Lord Stacy, I haven't gone there in weeks. I have my nails done at Rashine's now and on impulse decided to try Marco. *(Pats and smooths hair.)* How do you like it?

STACY: Looks like you slept in a rat's nest and gave up combing for Lent. Admit it Bonnie, you haven't been out of this house in two weeks. And judging from your clothes, probably not out of your bed.

BONNIE: So?

STACY: So — what's wrong?

BONNIE: Nothing's wrong. I know what worrywarts you and Mom are, so — lately, I've been a little tired and I've been catching up on my sleep, that's all.

STACY: *(Walks to her and feels forehead.)* Are you depressed that Ken is away on business?

BONNIE: No.

STACY: Then what's the matter? In all the years I've known you, you never once let yourself go like this. Never. Now tell me what's wrong.

1   **BONNIE:** I told you, it's nothing. Now leave me alone and

2   let me rest. *(Lays down, grabs bag of ice and puts it to her brow.)*

3   **STACY:** All right. Guess I'll have to call Ken and bring him

4   home early. *(Picks up phone.)*

5   **BONNIE:** *(Bolts upright.)* Don't you dare. And put down that

6   phone.

7   **STACY:** Going to talk? *(BONNIE looks away.)* OK. *(She starts to*

8   *dial.)*

9   **BONNIE:** Put it down, Stacy. I might as well tell you. You'll

10   find out soon enough anyway.

11   **STACY:** *(Hangs up.)* Find out what? Come on Bonnie, *(Sits*

12   *beside her)* I'm really concerned.

13   **BONNIE:** *(Beat)* Ken left me.

14   **STACY:** What? *(Slightly annoyed)* This better not be another

15   of your harebrained delusions.

16   **BONNIE:** It isn't.

17   **STACY:** But why? I thought you two were happy.

18   **BONNIE:** Happy is not a good word to describe Ken and me.

19   We were . . . content. Or at least, I thought we were.

20   **STACY:** I'm . . . surprised. Jeez Bonnie, *(Puts hand over*

21   *BONNIE's)* I know how upset you must be.

22   **BONNIE:** Oh, don't worry about me. *(Stands and starts pacing.)*

23   Worry about that bastard. After he finds out how much

24   I'm going to sue him for divorce, he won't be able to afford

25   tuna fish — let alone a new wife.

26   **STACY:** New wife? Ken left you for another woman?

27   **BONNIE:** Can you beat that? Ken is many things, but original

28   isn't one of them.

29   **STACY:** *(Slowly)* This doesn't sound like the Ken I know. Tell

30   me exactly what and *how* he told you.

31   **BONNIE:** What do you mean how? Like the worm he is.

32   *(Places hands over heart.)* "Bonnie — I don't know how to

33   say this, but . . . *(She walks to window.)*

34   **STACY:** *(Beat)* But . . . what?

35   **BONNIE:** *(Turns)* "but when I come back from my trip, it's

1 arrivederci". And then he had this leering grin on his
2 face, and said, "I'm gonna enjoy sleeping on ol' Gilda,
3 too." You know, you can live with a man for seven years
4 and still never really know him.
5 STACY: Gilda too?! I knew it! *(Jumps up.)* He was talking
6 about the boat he just bought — Gilda Two.
7 BONNIE: He never told me he bought a boat.
8 STACY: It was an anniversary surprise. Along with a trip to
9 Italy.
10 BONNIE: Isn't that just like Ken! He never could keep a
11 secret without dropping little hints.
12 STACY: You're hopeless! This time you really outdid yourself.
13 BONNIE: 'Course at the time I thought it very Freudian that
14 he would take up with a woman with the same name as
15 his mother. Oh Lord! I feel kind of foolish, sitting here
16 moping about this.
17 STACY: Good! Maybe now you'll learn to *think* before
18 jumping to your crazy conclusions. But I don't understand
19 something. Didn't Ken correct you when he realized you'd
20 misunderstood him?
21 BONNIE: *(Pause)* I don't think he realized it.
22 STACY: Why not?
23 BONNIE: Because when he told me — I said I hoped he'd finally
24 be happy. Then I walked into the bedroom and took a scissor
25 to all of his ties and left for a double feature. When I got back,
26 he was gone with a note attached to the bathroom mirror.
27 STACY: What did it say?
28 BONNIE: "You're cracked. If you wanted me to buy a new tie,
29 you could have told me."
30 STACY: Bonnie, I think you owe Ken an apology.
31 BONNIE: Me?! Don't be ridiculous. Ken should learn how to
32 keep secrets. After all, he gave me quite a scare. *(Looks*
33 *at watch.)* Look at the time — if I hurry I might be able to
34 catch Henrietta for a shampoo and blow dry. Make coffee
35 for me, will you? I'm going to jump into the shower. *(Exits)*

SCENE 12 — Charlotte and Betty
Age Level 20-40

SCENE OPENS: CHARLOTTE and BETTY are best friends. CHARLOTTE walks in from other room modeling her new dress.

CHARLOTTE: How do I look?

BETTY: Fantastic!

CHARLOTTE: Do I really? *(Goes to mirror.)* You don't think it's too fussy?

BETTY: Not at all. It's so chic, it looks like it was designed in Paris. Where'd you get it?

CHARLOTTE: *(Evasive)* I was in so many shops, I don't remember.

BETTY: Charlotte — you remember the number of links on a gold chain you saw three years ago. How much and where?

CHARLOTTE: I told you I don't remember. *(Turns back to mirror.)* Do you really think it's chic? I can hardly wait to show Cliff. He loves it when I look French.

BETTY: No he doesn't. You love it when you look French. He's just happy when you've stopped shopping.

CHARLOTTE: Then this dress will make him very happy. It should satisfy me for at least a month.

BETTY: *(Whistles)* That dress must have cost a fortune. How much?

CHARLOTTE: None of your business. Besides, we can afford it.

BETTY: No you can't. Cliff just got finished talking to you about a budget.

CHARLOTTE: Budget, smudget. He's beginning to sound like an old man. Believe me, Cliff makes enough money to feed all of Nairobi.

BETTY: There's something wrong if he can feed Nairobi, but not be able to clothe you. You've got to start thinking about your future.

1 CHARLOTTE: As far as I'm concerned — there's no future
2   worth thinking about if I have to go through it in tatters.
3 BETTY: There isn't a thing you own, that could be called
4   tattered. Not even your dog's raincoat or booties.
5 CHARLOTTE: You're beginning to sound like my mother —
6   and I don't appreciate it.
7 BETTY: Didn't you ever hear the story of the Ant and the
8   Grasshopper?
9 CHARLOTTE: Great. Now you're going to regale me with fairy
10   tales? Look Betty, spare me the "Save for a Rainy Day"
11   speech. Cliff has enough money to take care of Noah and
12   his Ark one thousand times the forty days. And if he
13   doesn't — then maybe he should start thinking about
14   making more now — before it's too late.
15 *(CHARLOTTE exits.)*
16
17
18
19
20
21
22
23
24
25
26
27
28
29
30
31
32
33
34
35

PART TWO:
Two Men

SCENE 13 — Brian and James

Age Level 18-23

SCENE OPENS: JAMES and BRIAN are brothers. They are
counting up their savings.

BRIAN: Jeez, I had no idea we had saved this much. How
much do you think it is?

JAMES: At least enough to buy a ten-speed. Maybe two.

BRIAN: Man, that's great! *(Pause)* How much is that?

JAMES: For a good one . . . about two hundred bucks. Makes
scrimping and saving all those months worth it.

BRIAN: Almost. I could have enjoyed going to that party
with Maureen.

JAMES: You still whining about that? Women. They're not
worth the time we spend thinking about them. If Maureen
really cared about you, she wouldn't have gone to that
stupid party with Cliff.

BRIAN: Yeah, I guess so. But still . . . I miss her.

JAMES: You miss her now . . . but once you're on your brand
new bike, flying with the wind — you're not going to give
her a second thought. I promise you that.

BRIAN: You promise lots of things that never come true.
I just hope you're right this time.

JAMES: Trust me, Bry. I've been there, so I know.

BRIAN: *(Beat)* I saw Kathy down at the drug store the other
day.

JAMES: So?

BRIAN: So — she said to say hi. You know, I never did know
what you and Kath fought about.

JAMES: Doesn't matter. What does matter is that you and I
are friends again. Just like old times.

BRIAN: Yeah. I never enjoyed fighting with you. You know
that.

JAMES: Sure I know it. But if you can't fight with your own

1   brother, who can you fight with?

2 BRIAN: Right! *(They give each other the high five sign.)* **What**

3   **kind of bike do you want to get?**

4 JAMES: I don't know. Maybe if we get secondhand bikes, we

5   can buy two.

6 BRIAN: Yeah! Then we can tool around together. Riding

7   cowboys looking for trouble.

8 JAMES: You're a nut. Listen, if we don't get two, and I'm

9   not keen on secondhand, then we're gonna have to decide

10   on — who gets which days to ride.

11 BRIAN: Which days? Well . . . I'd like Saturday. What do ya

12   say?

13 JAMES: No way.

14 BRIAN: Come on. I'll even take the three days out of the

15   seven, if I can have it on Saturday.

16 JAMES: Hey, forget it.

17 BRIAN: What do you mean, forget it? Somebody's got to have

18   Saturday.

19 JAMES: It was my idea to save. And if I wasn't on your

20   tail every second of every day, you would have blown the

21   money.

22 BRIAN: So what are you saying? You want Saturday?

23 JAMES: I'm saying . . . I deserve Saturday.

24 BRIAN: *(Beat)* OK. But then I get the extra day. Deal?

25 JAMES: What kind of a deal is that? I don't need to be penalized

26   just for *deserving* Saturday.

27 BRIAN: You are unbelievable. You don't deserve anything

28   except a lesson in how not to be selfish.

29 JAMES: No I don't. It's only right that I . . .

30 BRIAN: Right? You make me laugh.

31 JAMES: Let's not fight about this Brian. OK? We'll alternate

32   for the extra day.

33 BRIAN: I have a better idea. Let's forget the whole thing

34   and you give me my half of the money.

35 JAMES: Are you crazy? Buying a bike was the whole point

1   of saving these last few months.
2   BRIAN: Maybe for you. But the whole point for me was having
3   my brother back. Now — I'm not so sure I want him.
4   *(BRIAN exits.)*
5
6
7
8
9
10
11
12
13
14
15
16
17
18
19
20
21
22
23
24
25
26
27
28
29
30
31
32
33
34
35

SCENE 14 — Wade and Peter

Age Level 25-65

SCENE OPENS: WADE and PETER enter the room. WADE is a police detective. They are talking about PETER's sister-in-law Karen, who is living with PETER and his wife. PETER's failed attempt to kill Karen brought on Karen's amnesia and a suspicious detective. PETER wants to get rid of Karen before her memory returns.

PETER: So you can see my position.

WADE: Very clearly.

PETER: Good. Then we understand each other.

WADE: Absolutely.

PETER: Well?

WADE: Well, what?

PETER: Wade, I asked you here to get some feedback. Not to parrot me. What do you think I should do with her?

WADE: You've already made up your mind. So why ask me?

PETER: True. The decision *is* up to me.

WADE: The decision is up to Lisa, your wife. After all, Karen is her sister.

PETER: My wife is too emotional about this. She's not capable of making a sensible decision.

WADE: Then my feedback is — you should wait until she *can* make a sensible one.

PETER: I can't wait that long.

WADE: If you force Lisa to do something against her will concerning her sister . . . she'll resent you for the rest of her life.

PETER: She'll get over it. I have to act quickly here. Karen's slipping fast. She's having nightmares, she's paranoid about her food — she's driving me nuts.

WADE: Maybe *you* should go away. The rest might do you some good.

1	PETER:	Look Wade, I'm asking for your help. I need support
2		on this. Lisa respects you and will listen if you tell her
3		you agree with me.
4	WADE:	But I don't.
5	PETER:	Why not? Karen is acting crazy. It isn't normal to not
6		eat anything that isn't sealed in cans, plastic or glass and
7		insist on being present when they're opened. On second
8		thought, she's not acting crazy, she is.
9	WADE:	Maybe.
10	PETER:	What do you mean maybe?
11	WADE:	Peter — whatever happened to Karen the night I
12		found her on the cliffs was understandably traumatic.
13		Although we found no forced entry into your house, we
14		did find traces of someone else having been there.
15	PETER:	Lisa and I didn't even budge from our bedroom that
16		night let alone our section of the house.
17	WADE:	So you told us. That, coupled with the fact that the
18		maid had done her usual cleaning up that morning and ...
19	PETER:	Yes, yes. You already told me about the smudged
20		fingerprints from someone wearing gloves and the tread
21		of larger feet on the rug. So what?
22	WADE:	So that leaves us with a mystery. Karen's amnesia
23		leaves her only with the memory of the drink she had
24		with you and Lisa celebrating your anniversary. Who
25		else had been there that night?
26	PETER:	Who cares? With no evidence of Karen's having been
27		attacked other then the scrapes and bruises, which you
28		originally said happened as a result of a fall, why pursue
29		this idea of an attacker? I think it's just adding fuel to
30		her already paranoid fire.
31	WADE:	Let's just say — if she was drugged, and if she was
32		threatened, and if she was frightened for her life — that
33		could account for the state she's in right now. She needs
34		some time to settle down and feel safe again in order to
35		remember.

1 PETER: She can feel safe at that hospital. They have very
2   competent nurses and doctors who know what they're
3   doing.
4 WADE: Ordinarily, I would say you were right. But with
5   Karen's morbid fear of doctors, it could force her further
6   into herself — never to reawaken.
7 PETER: Well, what *I* don't need is to be reawakened at 3 a.m.
8   by a screaming banshee. I'm telling you Wade, it's fraying
9   my nerves.
10 WADE: You always said you had nerves of steel. Can't you
11   hang in there for just a little bit longer? At least for Lisa
12   if not for Karen?
13 PETER: No I can't. I have a business to run and I can't run it
14   when I don't get any sleep. Personally, I think it's having
15   a detrimental effect on Lisa too. Aren't you interested in
16   Lisa's welfare?
17 WADE: What I'm interested in is getting Karen's memory
18   back. We may not have hard-core evidence of an attack,
19   but I'm convinced that it happened. And I want to catch
20   the bastard. Don't you?
21 PETER: Of course I do. I'm all for justice being done, but at
22   what price? Lisa's future? Her happiness?
23 WADE: Lisa will be happy when Karen gets well. *(Beat)* If you
24   want, I'll talk with Lisa about her options.
25 PETER: Good. I think we should band together. Maybe we
26   could put Karen in a sanitarium instead of a hospital. No
27   white coats. No squeaky shoes. Just a lot of green space,
28   trees and quiet.
29 WADE: I'll think about it. I don't guarantee anything.
30 PETER: I don't need guarantees. I know you'll do the right
31   thing. *(Smiles)*
32 WADE: You can count on that. *(WADE exits.)*
33 PETER: *(Smile fades. To self)* No — I'll see to it. *(Goes to phone.)*
34
35

SCENE 15 — Chris and Evan
Age Level 18-30

SCENE OPENS: CHRIS and EVAN dislike each other intensely. CHRIS is visiting Holly who is his stepsister. He is also in love with her, though he doesn't admit it. The doorbell rings and CHRIS answers. It's EVAN.

CHRIS: Why can't you get this through your thick head? Holly is not interested in seeing you.

EVAN: Oh? What I'm not interested in is your opinion. *(Moves into room.)*

CHRIS: *(Blocking EVAN's progress)* She told me she never wanted to see you again.

EVAN: I want to hear her say that. Not you.

CHRIS: Look Pal. After what you pulled the last time you were with her, you should be happy she doesn't have you arrested.

EVAN: I had a reason for what I did. And you know something, pal, I think you had something to do with it.

CHRIS: Me? How could I have had something to do with your brawl?

EVAN: Someone left that message.

CHRIS: What message?

EVAN: You know damn well what message. I can't believe what a sucker I was. "Holly's being abducted. Come save her."

CHRIS: It should teach you not to be so impulsive. Anyway, that didn't give you the right to rush over and punch the guy in the nose, like some hoodlum.

EVAN: I didn't rush over. I walked. I also asked him to let go of her arm. He wouldn't, so I decked him. So what!

CHRIS: So what? You just lost yourself Holly.

EVAN: Get out of my way. *(Pushing past him)* Holly? Hey, Holly it's me. I'm real . . .

CHRIS: *(Grabs EVAN by his shirt.)* Look Pal . . . are you hard of

1   hearing? Or perhaps you respond best to sign language.

2   *(Holds up fist and threatens him.)*

3   EVAN: *(Brushing off hand)* **All I want to do is apologize to Holly.**

4   CHRIS: **So write her a note. I'll make sure she gets it.**

5   EVAN: **I just bet you will.**

6   CHRIS: **Listen chump. You blew it. And you know what? I**

7   **knew someday you'd hang yourself.**

8   EVAN: **With a little help from you. Where is she?**

9   CHRIS: **Privileged information.**

10 EVAN: **You know something, Chris? You're a privileged jerk.**

11 CHRIS: *(Sits down.)* **Sticks and stones.**

12 EVAN: *(Beat)* **OK. But nobody is going to keep me from finding**

13   **Holly and talking to her — least of all you.** *(Walks to door.)*

14 CHRIS: **Don't let the door hit you on the way out.**

15 EVAN: **After all this is over, Chris — I owe you one.**

16   *(EVAN exits.)*

17

18

19

20

21

22

23

24

25

26

27

28

29

30

31

32

33

34

35

SCENE 16 — Jake and Douglas
Age Level 20-65

SCENE OPENS: JAKE is sitting on the sofa with a drink in his hand. In his other, he holds a scarf. His father, DOUGLAS, enters.

DOUGLAS: **Drinking alone, Jake? Thought I always told you that was bad practice.**

JAKE: **So you did.** *(Takes sip.)*

DOUGLAS: *(Seeing his face)* **Something bothering you?** *(Goes to get self a scotch. Laughs to self.)* **Bet you had a hard day over at the tennis court. Lady beat you?**

JAKE: *(Beat)* **Yeah. You could say that.**

DOUGLAS: **I envy you your problems. Well, don't let it get you down. Some days are like that.**

JAKE: **How would you know? You've always told me, when you play — you play to win.**

DOUGLAS: **Doesn't mean I always do. In life you've got to accept the losses, learn from them, and go on. Just remember to never make the same mistake twice.**

JAKE: **The Harlon motto.**

DOUGLAS: **Right.**

JAKE: *(Beat)* **Dad? Do you remember Jocelyn McQue?**

DOUGLAS: **Sure. Pretty little thing. Married Endicott didn't she?**

JAKE: **Married and separated.**

DOUGLAS: **Really? Must have been quiet. I didn't hear anything about it. Maybe that's why Endicott's been giving me trouble.**

JAKE: **What kind of trouble?**

DOUGLAS: **Nothing I can't handle. Why?**

JAKE: *(Beat)* **I think I'm still in love with Jocelyn.**

DOUGLAS: **Still? What are you talking about?**

JAKE: **The month before Jocelyn and Endicott were married**

1   . . . the summer that she . . .

2 DOUGLAS: Hold it! I'm not going to hear something about

3   their baby, am I?

4 JAKE: Dad, we were in love.

5 DOUGLAS: For the love of God, Jake! You're talking about

6   Endicott. *The Endicotts!*

7 JAKE: Dad, she didn't love him. She never did.

8 DOUGLAS: Since when does that have anything to do with

9   the price of beans? Jesus! You could have ruined everything!

10   That marriage was planned, counted on and expected,

11   by half of the most influential people in this town.

12 JAKE: That's too damn bad about the people in this town.

13   What about Jocelyn? What about happiness?

14 DOUGLAS: Happiness is an acquired by-product of hard

15   work. She just didn't try hard enough.

16 JAKE: She did try. She was unhappy and didn't know what

17   to do.

18 DOUGLAS: You sticking your nose in where it didn't belong

19   — certainly didn't help matters.

20 JAKE: She still married him, didn't she? She still did what

21   everyone expected of her.

22 DOUGLAS: Everyone expects her to *stay* married and keep

23   the Endicott line going. Not extend the *Harlon* line.

24 JAKE: If I'd known she was carrying my child . . . I never

25   would have let her marry him.

26 DOUGLAS: Like hell you wouldn't. *(Beat)* Does Endicott

27   know it's not his child?

28 JAKE: No. At least I don't think so.

29 DOUGLAS: You listen to me, Jake, and listen good! Till this

30   blows over, you will stay away from Jocelyn and you'll

31   keep your distance from Endicott.

32 JAKE: I can't promise you that.

33 DOUGLAS: You better. Or by God I will personally see to it

34   that you are barred from every country club, restaurant,

35   social function . . .

1   JAKE: You don't have to threaten me. Jocelyn asked me not
2   to see her again. Not till she gets her priorities
3   straightened out.
4   DOUGLAS: Straightened out or not — you stay away from
5   her Jake, she's poison.
6   JAKE: You don't have to remind me that Endicott could kill
7   your political chances in this town — or anywhere for
8   that matter. But Dad . . . without Jocelyn — I'm half dead.
9   DOUGLAS: With Jocelyn — you'll make us *all dead.*
10   *(DOUGLAS exits.)*
11
12
13
14
15
16
17
18
19
20
21
22
23
24
25
26
27
28
29
30
31
32
33
34
35

SCENE 17 — Detrick and Russ
Age Level 25-65

SCENE OPENS: DETRICK is a private eye that was hired by
RUSS's aunt who is now dead. RUSS owns a caberet.

RUSS: **Come in.** *(As DETRICK starts in)* **Wipe your feet. My
wife's very fond of that Persian.**

DETRICK: *(Wiping feet carefully and enters)* **I'm glad you could
see me, Mr. Gordon. I don't think you'll be disappointed.**

RUSS: **I better not be. I cancelled a rehearsal today.**

DETRICK: **Yeah, I caught your show. Real nice moves.**

RUSS: **Thanks.**

DETRICK: **Must be hard getting good dancers with all the
same hair color.**

RUSS: **Those are wigs, Mr. Canarsey. Makes them appear
uniform. Helps with the act.**

DETRICK: **Oh, no kidding? Could have fooled me. Guess you
know lots of tricks like that.**

RUSS: **You could say that. My choreographer helps with the
overall concepts, but in my line of business, you learn to
make due with what you have.**

DETRICK: **You don't strike me as a man who'd make do.
More like a man who — gets things done.**

RUSS: *(Beat)* **What exactly is this piece of information you
have for me, Mr. Canarsey?**

DETRICK: **Detrick. But you can call me Deet.**

RUSS: **Deet. Get to the point.**

DETRICK: **Your Aunt Mildred Kennsington hired me before
she died.**

RUSS: **Why?**

DETRICK: **To make sure all her affairs were in order.**

RUSS: **A little out of your line, don't you think? You did say
you were a private investigator.**

DETRICK: **That's right. But actually, it turned out to be right**

– 48 –

1   **up my alley.**

2   **RUSS: And what alley is that?**

3   **DETRICK: The dead-end kind. Murder.**

4   **RUSS: Really? Whose murder?**

5   **DETRICK: Your aunt's.**

6   **RUSS: My aunt died from natural causes. The police report**

7   **says so.**

8   **DETRICK: Does it? I happen to know she was murdered.**

9   **RUSS: That's a pretty big statement. Have you gone to the**

10   **police with it?** *(Goes to couch.)*

11   **DETRICK: Not yet.** *(Follows him. Stands at corner.)* **Knowing**

12   **that you were her favorite nephew, I thought you might**

13   **be able to help me in my investigation.**

14   **RUSS: Why can't the police help you?**

15   **DETRICK: Someone was clever enough to murder her and**

16   **make it look like an accident. But they weren't clever**

17   **enough to dispose of the evidence.**

18   **RUSS: What evidence?**

19   **DETRICK: That's the point.** *(Sits next to RUSS.)* **I need you to**

20   **find it.**

21   **RUSS: ** *(Gets up and moves away.)* **What makes you think I know**

22   **where it is? I don't even know what you're talking about.**

23   **DETRICK: I need someone who knew your aunt better than I**

24   **did, to help me figure out what she did with it.**

25   **RUSS: Did with what, Mr. Canarsey?**

26   **DETRICK: Deet.**

27   **RUSS: How can I help you find something I don't know**

28   **anything about?**

29   **DETRICK: OK. Your aunt was afraid she might be murdered**

30   **and told me she would hide the evidence in the library.**

31   **Unfortunately, she never got the chance to tell me where**

32   **or what it was.**

33   **RUSS: I didn't realize my aunt was afraid of being murdered.**

34   **Did she say by whom?** *(Walks to chair and sits, slowly drinking*

35   *his drink.)*

1   DETRICK: No. She was very secretive about her suspicions.

2   RUSS: She was secretive about lots of things. The Old Crow.

3   DETRICK: Did she have any favorite places to hide things in?
4   A drawer? A hidden panel?

5   RUSS: Not that I know of.

6   DETRICK: She trusted you. Surely she must have told you
7   something.

8   RUSS: It would help if I knew what I was looking for.

9   DETRICK: Maybe I ought to go to the police and have them
10   shake down the whole room. They might come up with
11   something. *(Heads for door.)*

12   RUSS: *(Getting up)* I don't think that's such a good idea. After
13   all, it's a closed case now and I'd hate to have cops turning
14   my house upside down.

15   DETRICK: They would be very thorough.

16   RUSS: Look — why don't we try to find whatever she's hidden
17   by ourselves? That will mean a big coup for you. Heighten
18   your prestige, if we find it.

19   DETRICK: Yeah. And lessen your scandal, if the hunt pans out.

20   RUSS: I'm glad we understand each other. *(Pause)* I'm curious.
21   Why trust me?

22   DETRICK: Who says I do?

23   RUSS: Thanks.

24   DETRICK: I figured the odds. I had to trust someone from
25   this family, so I picked you.

26   RUSS: I should be flattered. Guess that means I'm less under
27   suspicion then everyone else. Right?

28   DETRICK: Wrong. You just have less motive. After all, your
29   wife inherited, not you.

30   RUSS: True. Lisa inherited everything. Every lock, stock and
31   barrel. *(Beat)* Care for a drink, Mr. ... Deet?

32   DETRICK: Thanks. Bourbon. No ice.

33   RUSS: A real drinking man. *(Gets drink, hands it to him and*
34   *sits.)* So Deet, you've intrigued me. You say there might
35   be damaging evidence in my aunt's library on who killed

1   **her. Why don't you tell me the whole story starting at the**
2   **beginning, and maybe we can figure out this puzzle**
3   **together.** *(Sees DETRICK finishing off drink. Gets up and*
4   *brings the bottle to table.)* **Here, have another.** *(He pours.)*
5
6
7
8
9
10
11
12
13
14
15
16
17
18
19
20
21
22
23
24
25
26
27
28
29
30
31
32
33
34
35

SCENE 18 — Josh and Greg

Age Level 25-50

SCENE OPENS: JOSH is an ex-con. GREG is a cop. Entrance of
JOSH. The warehouse is in semi-darkness and GREG is sitting
in a chair, slightly turned away from entrance, waiting.

JOSH: *(Whispering)* **Mary? Mary?** *(GREG gets up and JOSH sees
him.)* **What the hell are you doing here?**

GREG: **Nice to see you too, Josh.** *(As JOSH starts to leave)* **I
wouldn't try going anywhere if I were you.**

JOSH: **Oh? Who's going to stop me?**

GREG: **Don't ask a question we both know the answer to.**

JOSH: **Look Greg — you don't have anything on me.**

GREG: **How about the possibility of my foot across your
neck?** *(Beat)* **Sit down Josh, I've got a few things I want
to ask you.**

JOSH: **Maybe some other time. Right now, I'm in a big hurry.**

GREG: **Haste makes waste, Josh. You should know that.**
(Starts to edge toward him.)

JOSH: **Listen, Greg, you've got me all wrong.**

GREG: **I doubt that.**

JOSH: **I didn't steal anything and I certainly didn't set that
fire. Why don't you believe me?**

GREG: **Why? Because it's very hard to believe a cowardly
liar and thieving blackmailer.**

JOSH: **All fabrications. I was set up.**

GREG: **Like you set Mary up? Now,** *(Grabbing his arm he ushers
him toward the couch where he throws him down)* **let's have
that chat.**

JOSH: **Jesus, Greg. I think you broke my arm.**

GREG: **Just imagine how it will feel if I do.**

JOSH: **I didn't know you were so violent.**

GREG: **You should have taken the time to get to know me when
you had the chance. You could have saved yourself the**

1   trouble of finding out the hard way.

2 JOSH: Speaking of trouble, *(Tries to get up)* . . . if I don't get out

3   of here real soon, I'm going to be up to my neck in it.

4 GREG: *(Pushing him back down)* **Going to? You already are.**

5   So relax and let's start with the question, "Where's Mary"?

6 JOSH: Mary? I have no idea. She was supposed to meet me in

7   this warehouse over an hour ago.

8 GREG: Don't lie to me.

9 JOSH: I'm not lying. I swear to God, Greg.

10 GREG: Uh, oh. Whenever you start using God I know I'm in

11   trouble. Now try to focus on your priorities — like pain-

12   free bodily parts, and tell me where she is.

13 JOSH: You know what your problem is? You're too tense.

14   How 'bout you and me, we go for a drink and we can

15   talk . . .

16 GREG: Not this time. Last time we went for a drink you

17   slipped me a Mickey and it took two days to get rid of

18   the hangover.

19 JOSH: Are you still sore about that? I did it for your own

20   good. You would have gotten hurt if you had followed me.

21 GREG: Your concern gets me right here. *(Leaning very close to*

22   *him)* Read my lips, Josh. If you don't tell me where Mary

23   is, I'm going to break your fingers one by one, and then

24   I'll start on your toes. The pain lasts a long, long time

25   and sometimes . . . it never goes away.

26 JOSH: What are they doing down at the police station? Giving

27   Nazi lessons?

28 GREG: Come on Josh. Quit stalling.

29 JOSH: I'm not stalling. I honestly don't know where Mary is.

30   She was supposed to be here.

31 GREG: Supposed to be, but isn't. *(Beat)* If she's not here,

32   where else would she be.

33 JOSH: Don't know. She called me last night and told me to

34   meet her here and then hung up. That's all I know.

35 GREG: I've got to find her. And soon.

```
1   JOSH:   (Looking nerviously around) I don't know any more than
2           I already told you. Can I go now?
3   GREG:   Sure. We can both go.
4   JOSH:   Both? No way. Trust me on this Greg, I can't go with
5           you.
6   GREG:   Trust you? You and what snake.
7   JOSH:   Please, you're hurting my feelings. I'd like to help,
8           but right now is not a good time for me.
9   GREG:   Gee, that's too bad. (Grabs him and pushes him toward
10          the door.) And don't try any funny stuff. I've got very long
11          arms. (Just before leaving the room, GREG turns and looks
12          back.) Damn it Mary. Where the hell are you? (They exit.)
13
14
15
16
17
18
19
20
21
22
23
24
25
26
27
28
29
30
31
32
33
34
35
```

SCENE 19 — Roy and Craig
Age Level 17-35

SCENE OPENS: ROY and CRAIG are brothers. CRAIG has come to stay with ROY during the summer. ROY comes into the kitchen and finds CRAIG reading his mail.

ROY: *(Snatching the mail from CRAIG)* **How many times do I have to tell you — I don't want you reading my mail!**

CRAIG: **I was bored. Besides, don't leave what you don't want read on the kitchen table.**

ROY: *(Looking through the mail he comes across certain letters.)* **These were *not* on the kitchen table, they were ... you know Craig, you're becoming very irritating lately. Snooping into things that don't concern you.**

CRAIG: **Like what? Some crummy mail catalogues and cryptic letters? Big deal. I have as much right to browse through this house as you do.**

ROY: **Wrong. This is *my* house and you're supposed to be a guest.**

CRAIG: **Great! First you tell me to make myself at home and when I do — you throw it back in my face. Thanks a lot.**

ROY: **Common courtesy is expected everywhere.**

CRAIG: **You're overreacting. So I picked up something to read with my Cheerios™. So what?**

ROY: **Don't be a smart ass. You don't go rifling through people's dresser drawers to find suitable reading material for breakfast.**

CRAIG: **I swear — it was on the kitchen table.** *(Holds up hand.)* **Honest.**

ROY: **That does it. I can take a lot of things, but bald-faced lying from you isn't one of them. Call up Mom and tell her you're going home on the next flight out of here.**

CRAIG: **No way. You're not sending me packing ol' buddy, so get that thought out of your head.**

1	ROY:	Let me explain as briefly as I can — the circumstances
2		in which you came to live with me. One — Mom was ready to
3		send you to a summer camp they nick-named "Penitentiary
4		Hell Hole". Two — with my crazy hours and schedule I
5		needed someone to take care of Chester — you remember
6		him don't you? The little schnauzer with the sad eyes
7		and weak kidneys, and three — for some crazy reason I
8		thought that maybe, just maybe, you might have needed
9		to get out and be on your own. *(Sees his wallet lying on the*
10		*table, takes it and starts to put it in his back pocket. Stops and*
11		*looks inside of it instead.)* **With grown-up responsibilities.**
12		**Obviously, I was wrong.**
13	CRAIG:	OK, so I'll walk Chester more often. I've been busy.
14	ROY:	I'll bet you have.
15	CRAIG:	What does that mean?
16	ROY:	I may appear absent-minded once in a while — but
17		stupid I'm not. Somehow, between last night and this
18		morning, I must have spent another twenty dollars.
19	CRAIG:	Living in Manhattan can be mighty expensive.
20	ROY:	I had eighty dollars when I went to sleep — and I
21		haven't been out this morning yet.
22	CRAIG:	So?
23	ROY:	So — start packing. *(Heads toward door.)*
24	CRAIG:	Oh, Roy. Should I pack the photographs too? I'll be
25		kind of bored on the plane and might need something to
26		occupy me.
27	ROY:	*(Stopped dead in his tracks. Turns and stares at CRAIG.)*
28		What photographs?
29	CRAIG:	Oh. Didn't I tell you? Guess it slipped my mind. You
30		received a package today from a Mr. uh ... Dray
31		*(Snapping finger)* I think it was. Special delivery. Didn't
32		want to wake you when it came.
33	ROY:	Why you little bastard. *(Going to him)* Give them to me.
34	CRAIG:	Say please. Mom's very particular about the social
35		amenities. *(Tsk Tsk's)* Living along can wreak havoc on

1   basic manners.
2 ROY: Craig — you don't understand what those pictures
3   represent. I suggest you give them to me before you end
4   up in some serious hot water.
5 CRAIG: Gee big brother, you're scaring me. What kind of hot
6   water and how much does it mean in cold hard cash?
7 ROY: *(Laughs)* You stupid . . . maybe I *should* let you keep
8   them. *(Walks to door.)* Those pictures had better be on the
9   table when I get back. No negotiations. No nothing. This
10   time, you might have bitten off a little more than even
11   you can chew.
12 CRAIG: I've got a big appetite.
13 ROY: Half an hour. *(ROY exits.)*
14 CRAIG: Don't bet on it.
15
16
17
18
19
20
21
22
23
24
25
26
27
28
29
30
31
32
33
34
35

SCENE 20 — Tom and Rob
Age Level 25-35

SCENE OPENS: ROB is sitting at bar waiting for his best friend, TOM, to show up. He's been disappointed by TOM either not showing or not making any time for him and their friendship. He hopes this time will be different. Strains from the juke box can be heard. TOM enters.

TOM: Hey RB, what's happening? *(They greet each other with a high five sign.)* **Been here long?**

ROB: Nope. Just long enough for a cold one.

TOM: I'd better catch up then. *(To bartender)* **One beer please. Extra frosty glass.** *(Turns back to ROB.)* **Hey my man,** *(Pounds him on the back)* **long time no see.**

ROB: Not by my choice.

TOM: True. I've been real busy.

ROB: So you've told me.

TOM: No really. Work — plus the biddy is bustin' my butt. In fact, can't stay long tonight.

ROB: Oh great! Tom, this was supposed to make up for the night you left me last time. I haven't seen you in months.

TOM: Don't worry. I'm being a good boy getting in early tonight, so Chrissy won't have nothing to say the next time.

ROB: Good boy? What are you, a child?

TOM: *(Explaining)* **Look — if I get home early tonight, when we go out next time — I can stay out a whole lot longer.**

ROB: Within reason, you mean. Last time we were out you said the same thing, and you left by eleven.

TOM: Chrissy claims I wake her up if I come in later than that. Then she starts hasslin' me and believe me buddy — it's not worth it. *(At ROB's annoyance)* **Don't worry, I've got a plan. Like I said, I'm gonna score points with Chris by getting in early tonight. This way she won't say no**

1   the next time.
2   ROB: Bull. She says no every time. Besides, scoring points
3   should happen in a basketball game, not a marriage.
4   TOM: Gimme a break, Rob. You don't know Chrissy when she
5   gets on a roll. She's murder.
6   ROB: Tom — we've been best friends for as long as I can
7   remember. I got ta tell you pal, I'm not happy. I *never* get
8   to see you anymore. You never come down to play ball . . .
9   TOM: Chrissy likes to go shopping on the weekends.
10   ROB: Hell man. Can't you shop *after* ball?
11   TOM: She gets uptight Rob. What am I gonna do?
12   ROB: Tell her "too damn bad". Tell her that you have a right
13   to some time for yourself and your friends. It's not all
14   that often you know.
15   TOM: OK. Maybe if I tell her this Saturday is a big
16   championship game or something and you need me down
17   at the . . .
18   ROB: *(Disgusted)* Screw the schemes, Tom. Come down and
19   play ball once in a while. Can't you tell her you'll take
20   the kids when you get home and let her go out by herself
21   if she wants?
22   TOM: Tried that, but no way. She likes to sleep late on
23   Saturdays and I usually have to keep them busy.
24   ROB: Perfect. Then pack the kids up and bring them. Take
25   some toys and they can play down at the gym.
26   TOM: I don't know. She'll probably have something to say
27   about that too.
28   ROB: Like what? What could she possibly have to say except,
29   thanks for the peace and quiet.
30   TOM: You know her, Rob. She'll say if I play on Saturdays
31   and see my friends, then I can't go out for my Boys Nights
32   Out. And I love my BNO's.
33   ROB: One thing has nothing to do with the other. Stand up
34   to her like a man. You need to see friends, not just family
35   all the time.

1   TOM: Chrissy doesn't see it like that. Look, let's talk about
2   something else.
3   ROB: You mean you're not willing to *make* her see it that
4   way.
5   TOM: *(Beat)* Yeah. I guess if you put it that way.
6   ROB: *(Pause)* So — you're willing to let, what I call our
7   friendship, die.
8   TOM: I'm not saying that. We just can't see each other as
9   much as we used to, that's all.
10   ROB: As much? Four times a year isn't as much. It's never.
11   TOM: Easy for you to say. You just don't understand. You're
12   lucky. Sue's not like that and besides, you don't have
13   kids. *(TOM sips beer.)*
14   ROB: *(Beat)* And you don't have any backbone. *(Stands up and*
15   *throws money down on the bar.)* When you turn into a
16   married man and not some little boy with a mother
17   fixation — give me a call. *(ROB exits.)*
18
19
20
21
22
23
24
25
26
27
28
29
30
31
32
33
34
35

SCENE 21 — Harry and Roy
Age Level 25-55

SCENE OPENS: HARRY and ROY are cops working on a case
together. ROY is in the apartment when HARRY bursts in.

HARRY: **What do you mean gone? That's impossible!** *(Pushes
past ROY.)

ROY: **I already checked, Harry. He's not here.**

HARRY: **Damn! I left my post for only twenty minutes. What
happened?**

ROY: **What do you think? He must have recognized you from
the window and bolted.**

HARRY: **No way.** *(Beat)* **Unless . . .**

ROY: **Unless what?!**

HARRY: **Sharon took some pictures of me at the beach.**

ROY: **Oh great! And you let her keep them?**

HARRY: **She's sentimental.**

ROY: **Chief's gonna love hearing that. "But the prostitute
was sentimental" you understand.**

HARRY: **Roy, I was squinting in the sun. My own mother
wouldn't recognize me.**

ROY: **We're not talking about your mother.** *(Annoyed)* **You're
the biggest screw-up I ever met. Why I let myself get stuck
with you, I'll never know.**

HARRY: **What do you mean stuck?** *I* **was the one that busted
his chops making a case that would stick this time and
included you in.**

ROY: **Thanks a lot. Great collar but whoops, no thanks. And
this isn't the first time you've blown something big.**

HARRY: **That wasn't my fault. The Anderson case was tipped
by someone.** *(Confidentially)* **And between you and me, I
think it was internal.**

ROY: **It was. You.**

HARRY: *(Surprised)* **That's a damn lie and you know it.**

1   **ROY:**   Do I? Personally, Harry, your record lately is making
2   me wonder whose side you're really on.
3   **HARRY:**   Take that back. *(Beat)* **Roy, so help me** ... *(Starts*
4   *menacingly toward him.)*
5   **ROY:**   What? You'll punch me out? I'd like to see you try.
6   *(They go face to face.)*
7   **HARRY:** *(Beat)* **Ahhhh, you're not worth it.** *(Walks to door.)*
8   **I'm gonna find Nichols. But this time by myself. For all I**
9   **know, *you* could have blown this — not me.** *(Exits)*
10   **ROY:** *(Calling after him)* **Yeah, yeah.** *(Loudly)* **Screw-up!** *(Beat.*
11   *Goes to phone and dials.)* **It's me. Look, you're off the hook,**
12   **but this time stay the hell away from him. You got that?!**
13   **I'm not covering for you again.** *(Pause)* **Yeah, same to you,**
14   **pal.** *(Hangs up. Exits)*
15
16
17
18
19
20
21
22
23
24
25
26
27
28
29
30
31
32
33
34
35

1

SCENE 22 — Ferris and Austin
Age Level 18-28
3

4   ***SCENE OPENS:***   FERRIS enters apartment with grocery bag in
5   hand. He enters singing.

6

7   **FERRIS:**   **"If you've got the time, we've got the beer, . . . "**
8   **AUSTIN:**   **Did you get it?**
9   **FERRIS:**   **'Course. When Ferris Grand wants something —**
10   **he gets it.**
11   **AUSTIN:**   **No problems?**
12   **FERRIS:**   **Does this face look like it had problems? Don't**
13   **worry Austin, you're sitting pretty.**
14   **AUSTIN:**   *(Gets up and walks to bag.)* **I'm not worried about**
15   **sitting.** *(Looks inside and pulls out six-pack.)* **Where's the**
16   **book?**
17   **FERRIS:**   *(Reaches into back pocket and pulls out small address*
18   *book.)* **Right here, champ.** *(AUSTIN grabs it out of his hand.)*
19   **Hey, you don't have to grab it.**
20   **AUSTIN:**   *(Leafing through it)* **You idiot! You got the wrong one.**
21   **FERRIS:**   **Don't call me that.** *(Slight pause. Then goes to book.)*
22   **What do you mean wrong one?! I got the only one.**
23   **AUSTIN:**   **I can't believe it. I trust you with one lousy, stupid**
24   **errand and you blow it!**
25   **FERRIS:**   **I didn't blow anything! You said her end table to**
26   **the left. I opened the drawer, saw the book — black like**
27   **you said — and pinched it.**
28   **AUSTIN:**   **I said the *bedroom* to the left — end table as you**
29   **walk in.** *(Throws book at him.)* **This is her brother's, you**
30   **moron.**
31   **FERRIS:**   **Her brother's?** *(Picks it up and looks through.)* **You**
32   **sure?**
33   **AUSTIN:**   **No. I made it up. You took the wrong one! What the**
34   **hell am I gonna do now?**
35   **FERRIS:**   **I can go right back and . . .**

1	AUSTIN:	. . . and get caught! You cut the alarm like I said,
2		didn't you?
3	FERRIS:	Yeah. But . . .
4	AUSTIN:	But nothing! How long do you think they're not
5		going to notice the little light blinking? How long before
6		they notice the wind whipping through the blinds in the
7		library?
8	FERRIS:	Maybe . . .
9	AUSTIN:	Ferris! These people have routines. They're
10		creatures of habit. I'd give them another half hour to get
11		through cocktails before they start wandering around.
12		That alarm's gonna be put through soon.
13	FERRIS:	Maybe not. I cut the phone wires too.
14	AUSTIN:	So they'll go to a neighbor's, idiot.
15	FERRIS:	I asked you before not to call me that! Besides, the
16		nearest neighbor is two miles away.
17	AUSTIN:	So?
18	FERRIS:	So I also took care of the cars. No fast way out.
19	AUSTIN:	They're stranded?
20	FERRIS:	Like fish out of water. Like two men in an igloo.
21		Like . . .
22	AUSTIN:	OK, Ferris. You made your point. *(Walks to couch.)*
23		This is good. Very good. It gives us a little leeway. How
24		long did it take you to get there?
25	FERRIS:	Fifteen minutes.
26	AUSTIN:	Fifteen minutes to get there. Five to get back in. I
27		think maybe we might still have a shot. Let's go. *(Grabs*
28		*jacket and heads for door.)*
29	FERRIS:	No.
30	AUSTIN:	What do ya mean, no? Come on.
31	FERRIS:	*(Stands reluctantly at table, pushing bag around.)* You
32		called me an idiot. I don't like that.
33	AUSTIN:	Well, sometimes you are — like now. So come on.
34		*(He doesn't move. AUSTIN to self)* Jeez, what a . . . OK Ferris,
35		I apologize. OK?

1	FERRIS: But you don't mean it. Say it like you mean it.
2	AUSTIN: *(Exasperated)* **Hmmmmmm!** *(Forced control)* **OK,**
3	**Ferris. I was being a jerk and I apologize. And this time,**
4	**I really mean it. OK?**
5	FERRIS: **OK. But don't call me that, anymore. I don't like it,**
6	**Austin. I don't.**
7	AUSTIN: **Let's talk about it in the car, all right!** *(Leaves)*
8	FERRIS: **All right. I just don't like it when you call me that,**
9	*(Exits)* **that's all.**
10	
11	
12	
13	
14	
15	
16	
17	
18	
19	
20	
21	
22	
23	
24	
25	
26	
27	
28	
29	
30	
31	
32	
33	
34	
35	

SCENE 23 — Trent and Mac

Age Level 19-28

SCENE OPENS: TRENT and MAC are work friends. They are in MAC's apartment getting ready for a double date.

TRENT: Will you hurry up? We're going to be late.

MAC: *(Walks out combing hair.)* Relax, we've got another hour at least.

TRENT: I just don't want to keep them waiting again. That's all.

MAC: You crack me up. It's like you're on your first date, or something.

TRENT: Oh, that's right. After you know someone, you can be rude and keep them waiting. Just not on the first date. Might tip them to your real personality.

MAC: You're a regular comedian, Trent. What I mean is, you don't have to be as uptight. You already know they like you, so you can relax. Look, why don't you get yourself a beer.

TRENT: *(Gets up and goes to refrigerator)* You want one?

MAC: Sure.

TRENT: *(He tosses MAC the beer and they open them together. TRENT spills some on his clothes.)* Oh, great. Now I'm gonna smell like an alcoholic.

MAC: No big deal. It'll remind her of her father.

TRENT: Eileen's father's a drunk?

MAC: Was. He died.

TRENT: I didn't know that. So Mr. Malcolm is her step-dad?

MAC: Yep. *(During exchange MAC is getting ready.)*

TRENT: You know her family pretty well. What are they really like?

MAC: OK. Mother's a saint. Sisters are all cute. Especially Emily. She's a real looker.

TRENT: How long have you known them?

1   MAC: Few years.

2   TRENT: You were friends with her brother, Joe, first. Right?

3   MAC: What is this? An inquisition?

4   TRENT: No. Just like to know how well you and Eileen know
5   each other. That's all.

6   MAC: Well enough to know she's a great girl. And you're
7   lucky she likes you. She doesn't like everybody, you know.

8   TRENT: Oh, no? Who doesn't she like?

9   MAC: Most of the big mouths down at Harley's. They're a
10   bunch of jerks anyway.

11 TRENT: *(Beat)* Did you ever date Eileen?

12 MAC: Sure. We were childhood sweethearts. But then she
13   gave me the ax.

14 TRENT: How come?

15 MAC: Trent — you're making me real tired, asking all these
16   questions. Why don't you save them up and ask Eileen.
17   OK?

18 TRENT: OK. Didn't know you were so sensitive.

19 MAC: I'm not sensitive. Just busy — as in trying to get ready
20   for our double date. Have you seen my black shoes?

21 TRENT: Under the chair. So Eileen called it quits?

22 MAC: That's right. *(Sits and puts on shoes.)* I was too wild for
23   her. I'll tell you something though. If I had to do it all
24   over again, I'd sing a different tune.

25 TRENT: You're still interested? Then why set me up? Why
26   not ask her out again?

27 MAC: I did. But as in the song, there's a time to reap and a
28   time to sow. As far as she's concerned, our time had come
29   and — it had gone. Then you came along. And she flipped.

30 TRENT: She did? Really?

31 MAC: Suppose I shouldn't have told you, huh? Ahh — girls
32   stick together, what the hell. Yeah, she's crazy about you.

33 TRENT: That's great. I don't mind telling you Mac, I'm crazy
34   about her too. She's so beautiful.

35 MAC: And smart. Remember that. She likes to be appreciated

1   for her brains too. Kind of sensitive about it.

2   TRENT: Sure, sure. And what a bod. It goes on forever.

3   MAC: Tell me about it.

4   TRENT: *(Pause)* Hey Mac — did you and Eileen ever . . . you
5   know.

6   MAC: Yeah I know. *(Angry and gets up)* And you should know I
7   don't kiss and tell. Got that?! And neither should you.

8   TRENT: Hey don't get sore. It's just a question.

9   MAC: The kind of question that the low lifes down at Harley's
10   ask. I thought you were different, Trent.

11   TRENT: Just guy talk for Chrisake. What are you so touchy
12   for?

13   MAC: *(Beat)* Might as well get this out now. If you hurt Eileen
14   in any way, Trent — you're gonna pay for it. I introduced
15   Eileen to you 'cause I thought you were different. Someone
16   she could talk to, good family. Someone who wouldn't
17   just be interested in her body.

18   TRENT: I am Mac. Take it easy.

19   MAC: *(Beat)* OK. But if you blow this one, consider yourself
20   a loser — cause once I get another shot, I'm not letting
21   her get away so easy. *(Grabs coat and leaves.)* Come on, I
22   think we're gonna be late.

23   TRENT: *(Follows him.)* Oh great!

24

25

26

27

28

29

30

31

32

33

34

35

SCENE 24 — Billy and Gordon
Age Level 15-18

SCENE OPENS: BILLY is sitting down on bench, outside principal's office, arms crossed. He's a large kid, popular around school, usually in trouble with the teachers. GORDON arrives carrying books and sits down next to him. He wears glasses and is small.

BILLY: **Oh great!** *(Calling out to school secretary)* **Couldn't you have found me a better inmate?** *(Moment)* **OK, Gordon, whatcha in for? Dissecting frogs and liking it?** *(Laughs at joke.)*

GORDON: **That's interesting. You used a big word and seemed to understand it.**

BILLY: **Hey twerp. How would you like a black eye?**

GORDON: **I wouldn't chance it if I were you. Might mess up your throwing arm.**

BILLY: **Moron** *(Beat. He's antsy.)* **So — looks like we're stuck here together. What do you wanna talk about? Nuclear fission?**

GORDON: **Here's an original thought. Why don't we just ignore each other.**

BILLY: **Fine with me.** *(Beat. Nervous)* **It's my third time this year. What do you think they're gonna do to me?**

GORDON: **Probably expel you. Have your parents down for intense meetings. No more ball. No more girls. No more friends.**

BILLY: **Jeez. All I did was make a perfect basket in Harmon's class.**

GORDON: **Harmon teaches English. Where'd you find a basketball hoop?**

BILLY: **In the trash can, numbskull. I aced a perfect bank shot.** *(Imitates shot.)* **Bang!**

GORDON: **Real cool, Billy. You trashed your entire future for a bank shot.** *(Laughs uproariously at joke.)* **Get it?**

1   Trashed — bank shot.

2 BILLY: Yeah, I got it. *(Stands up.)* Hey warden — I want out of

3   here. *(Starts to pace.)*

4 GORDON: I think they're busy. Probably pulling your

5   records and sticking pins in them.

6 BILLY: Knock it off, Gordon. They're not gonna throw me

7   out because of some stupid paper trick. So lay off. *(Silence)*

8   What're you here for, Einstein?

9 GORDON: Nothing. Thought I'd come down and see how the

10   other half lives.

11 BILLY: Other half this. *(Grabs him by the shirt front and lifts him*

12   *up.)* Ahhh, you're not worth the trouble I'd get in,

13   pounding you a couple of times. *(Drops him.)*

14 GORDON: How relieved I am you're so sensible. *(Straightens*

15   *his shirt. Beat)* What do they usually do to you for a first

16   offense?

17 BILLY: *(Pause)* Well, first — they take you inside, and ask you

18   to put your fingers on the corner of the desk. Then they

19   take a big ruler and . . .

20 GORDON: Liar. Corporal punishment went out a long time

21   ago.

22 BILLY: OK, don't believe me. First time I went in, took a week

23   to move my middle finger. Now, *(Holding it up)* it works

24   just fine.

25 GORDON: Jerk. *(Gets up and starts pacing.)* Besides, they

26   wouldn't dare. My father would be here in a flash.

27 BILLY: With trouble kids, they don't care. They write down

28   on your school chart that you fell down, or something.

29   Then, if you make a fuss, they put you down as a liar.

30 GORDON: So?! So let them. *(Sits)* I don't care anymore. *(Looks*

31   *very depressed.)*

32 BILLY: *(Takes pity on him.)* Ahhh — forget it. They just lecture

33   you. Sometimes I wish they would hit me and get it over

34   with.

35 GORDON: Think they'll tell my parents?

1   BILLY: Depends on what you're in for. What'd you do?

2   GORDON: I . . . punched Alvin in the face, and Miss Torey
3   saw me.

4   BILLY: Moose Carter? *(Shakes head.)* **Wow. You just signed**
5   **your death warrant Gord. Moose still believes in corporal**
6   **punishment.**

7   GORDON: One has to stand up for what's right.

8   BILLY: Which was? *(Silence)* **Come on, tell me. It'll be all over**
9   school soon anyway.

10   GORDON: He was harassing Jennifer Borray and she didn't
11   like it. So I said something, and then he called my mother
12   a nasty word and I . . . punched him.

13   BILLY: Wow! This is great. Even *I* wouldn't punch Moose
14   Carter. Not that I wouldn't like to. He's a jerk.

15   GORDON: My sentiments exactly.

16   BILLY: You must like Jennifer a whole bunch, buddy. You
17   can kiss your bones good-bye.

18   GORDON: *(Hesitates)* **Ahhh . . . wouldn't know of any — back**
19   way out of school would you?

20   BILLY: Nothing secret that nobody else knows about. Hey,
21   don't worry. Moose will probably deck you a couple of
22   times to prove himself, then get on with his life.

23   GORDON: Thanks, Billy, that makes me feel much better.

24   BILLY: Hey, I have an idea. Why don't you make a bomb in
25   science lab and blow him up. Nobody would blame you.

26   GORDON: Moose is tough. I'd have a better chance of escaping,
27   by blowing myself up.

28   BILLY: Protecting Jennifer's honor. I like that.

29   GORDON: I like Jennifer.

30   BILLY: Me too. Hey look, you're pretty smart in English.
31   Right?

32   GORDON: Yeah . . .

33   BILLY: Well, how about if you help me understand English —
34   and I give you some muscle protection?

35   GORDON: You mean tutor you?

1	BILLY: Yeah. See — the perfect bank shot was also an English
2	exam. I couldn't do it, so I decided to play cute and get
3	kicked out before they found out. So what do you say?
4	GORDON: *(Excited)* **Are you kidding? I'll even take the test**
5	**for you. But I thought you were afraid of Moose.**
6	BILLY: **I may not know English, but I know when to stay**
7	**away from trouble. Besides, Moose and I have been**
8	**needing to settle a few scores. Hopefully, it won't come**
9	**to anything. Just a lot of hot air.**
10	GORDON: **Thanks, Billy.** *(Perks up and digs in pocket.)* **Want**
11	**some gum?**
12	BILLY: **Hey! What are you, a juvenile delinquent? You know**
13	**gum isn't allowed in school.** *(Takes piece and they smile.)*
14	
15	
16	
17	
18	
19	
20	
21	
22	
23	
24	
25	
26	
27	
28	
29	
30	
31	
32	
33	
34	
35	

PART THREE:
Man and Woman

SCENE 25 — James and Krystal
Age Level 25-35

SCENE OPENS: JAMES and KRYSTAL are brother and sister.
Their father has just died and JAMES has come to offer her a
part of the inheritance if she complies with a few rules. He has
a briefcase in his hand.

JAMES: Now that I'm the head of the family — I think we
ought to get a few things straightened out.

KRYSTAL: By all means. I'm still surprised that Dad made
you the sole heir of his estate, though I'm not shocked.
His belief in your "essential fairness" was rock solid.

JAMES: Dear ol' Dad. I'm going to miss him.

KRYSTAL: Oh spare me.

JAMES: What? Don't you believe that I can grieve for my
own father?

KRYSTAL: If I didn't know you were one hundred miles away
at the time . . . I would have sworn you'd pushed him.

JAMES: OK. Under these sad circumstances, I was hoping
this meeting would be more pleasant. Obviously, you've
managed to put your grief behind you. I admire the fact
that you never seem to lack emotional fortitude.

KRYSTAL: James, I don't have time for your games or your
flattery. So let's get on with it.

JAMES: The only thing you do lack is patience. If you'd
played Dad for all he was worth — you might be in my
position right now.

KRYSTAL: I don't believe in manipulating people to get what
I want. I loved Dad. What he wanted done with his money
was his business.

JAMES: And I made it mine. *(Looking through briefcase)* **Now, I
have a contract here that allows you all the money you
need — up to five thousand dollars a month — with the
stipulation that you come back to Oakwood Manor and**

1   live with Penny and me. All you have to do is sign it.

2 KRYSTAL: You know damn well I won't sign that thing.

3 JAMES: Why not? I think I'm being fair. After all, a family
4   should . . . stick together.

5 KRYSTAL: I told you the night I moved out — I would never
6   sleep under the same roof with you again.

7 JAMES: I wasn't thinking of you necessarily . . . sleeping.

8 KRYSTAL: You really disgust me. I can't believe how
9   innocent and pure you look on the outside when you're —
10   Mom and Dad never saw it either. They just believed you
11   every time you'd smile, open your big blue eyes and then
12   lie through your teeth.

13 JAMES: They were foolish and stupid. Remember when they
14   caught me smothering the kittens? *(Starts to smile at the*
15   *remembrance.)* Four were dead and one was scratching to
16   get out from under the pillow, and I told them I wanted to
17   see the angels take them away — that I didn't understand
18   what dead was. 'Course I was only ten so they believed . . .

19 KRYSTAL: I remember. I remember that vividly. I laid awake
20   for three nights, terrified you'd do that to me.

21 JAMES: *(Goes to touch her.)* No. I had never wanted to smother
22   you Krystal.

23 KRYSTAL: *(Moving away from him)* Look James — you can't
24   force me to move back to Oakwood, even if you manage
25   to cut me off without a penny. I'd rather starve.

26 JAMES: Interesting choice of words. Speaking of Penny, I'm
27   thinking of bringing her home from boarding school — so
28   we can all be one big happy family again.

29 KRYSTAL: But Penny's crazy about that school. She's made
30   lots of friends, the teachers adore her . . .

31 JAMES: Well if you don't come to stay with me, I'll be terribly
32   lonely. I'll have to have someone to . . . talk to.

33 KRYSTAL: You are so self-centered. What kind of company
34   could a fifteen year old . . . *(Realization)* not Penny!

35 JAMES: Relax. Penny will stay at school, far away. What I'm

1	interested in, is you. I've always wanted us to be closer,
2	Krystal. This would be the perfect time. *(Starts moving*
3	*toward her.)* No parents around. No bratty little sister.
4	Just you and me and all that money. Think of it. Heaven
5	right here on earth.
6	KRYSTAL: *(Moving away)* You mean Hell. I couldn't imagine
7	anything more horrible than to be alone with you. *(Turns*
8	*away.)* You make me sick.
9	JAMES: *(Coming up behind her)* Krystal, *(Takes her by the shoulders.*
10	*Both facing front or at angle. An over the shoulder shot)* think
11	back to happier times. There were fun times we had. The
12	time up at the lake. And the weekends during the
13	summers. *(Pulls her into him.)* We belong together.
14	KRYSTAL: *(Breaking free)* Let go of me. I never, never forgave
15	myself for those sordid, disgusting . . .
16	JAMES: Oh, come on. You had as much fun as I did.
17	KRYSTAL: You blackmailed me! Well, *(Walks to contract, picks*
18	*it up and throws it at him)* it's not going to happen again.
19	JAMES: It's just a matter of knowing which buttons to push.
20	*(Picks up contract.)*
21	KRYSTAL: You *would* think that money was everybody's
22	button. But this time, you miscalculated. This is the last
23	time I make the mistake of meeting you. Get out.
24	JAMES: *(Gathers briefcase. At door he turns and says)* Ah, Krystal
25	. . . Penny and I will miss you.
26	KRYSTAL: You wouldn't.
27	JAMES: I'll just leave the contract here *(Puts down on table.)*
28	— so you can think about it. *(At door he turns and says)* Bye
29	sis. *(He blows her a kiss. JAMES exits.)*
30	
31	
32	
33	
34	
35	

SCENE 26 — Brian and Kathy

Age Level 20-35

SCENE OPENS: BRIAN and KATHY are friends. He is very
muscular — the body beautiful type. She is very petite. The
bell rings and KATHY answers it.

BRIAN: What luck — you are home.

KATHY: Yep. I'm home. *(She lets him in.)*

BRIAN: Something wrong?

KATHY: No. Just feeling a little sorry for myself.

BRIAN: Then cheer up. How would you like to go to my brother's
wedding with me?

KATHY: Me? Don't be silly.

BRIAN: I'm not.

KATHY: I couldn't. *We* couldn't.

BRIAN: Why?

KATHY: Because . . . we'd look ridiculous — like Mutt and
Jeff going to a dance together. *(Eyeing him)* Only a Jeff
who's been on super vitamins.

BRIAN: We wouldn't have to dance, if you'd rather not.

KATHY: No thanks. Don't look at me like that. I hate weddings.
Besides, what would we talk about? The new issue of
Body by Nautilus?

BRIAN: Thanks! *(Goes to leave, but turns back at door.)* You know,
I'm sick and tired of people thinking that my muscles are
indicative of what's going on in my mind. I'm not an
overgrown, brainless jock whose entire vocabulary is
"uh, workout — uh, biceps".

KATHY: I'm sorry, Brian. Sometimes my jokes are not very
well timed. If you were in a better mood, you would have
laughed.

BRIAN: If you were in a better mood — you wouldn't have
made fun of me.

KATHY: Touché. And you're right. Here, *(She hands him a couch*

1   *pillow)* **beat me to a pulp.**

2 **BRIAN:** **I'd rather that you went to the wedding.**

3 **KATHY:** **Tricky, very tricky. But I don't think so.** *(At his silence)*

4   **I'm not going to add to the reason why, if that's what**

5   **you're waiting for.**

6 **BRIAN:** **I deserve an explanation.** *(Beat)* **If you can't think of**

7   **one, then lie.**

8 **KATHY:** *(Considers, then gives in.)* **OK. When I broke up with**

9   **Rick, I decided not to date, even friends, before I can**

10   **think through what happened.**

11 **BRIAN:** **Think it through after the wedding. Besides, Rick**

12   **was a jerk and doesn't deserve you wasting time, thinking**

13   **about him.**

14 **KATHY:** **Hey — I thought you liked him.**

15 **BRIAN:** **I liked you. He just happened to be a necessary part**

16   **of being around you.**

17 **KATHY:** *(Surprised)* **Brian, stop joking around.**

18 **BRIAN:** **You know Kath . . . for someone who likes to tell**

19   **jokes, I'm surprised you can't tell the difference between**

20   **joking and someone telling you the truth.**

21 **KATHY:** **I . . . I don't know what to say.**

22 **BRIAN:** **Say yes. I'd love to go to your brother's wedding.**

23 **KATHY:** **You and I are** *friends*, **Brian. I've never even**

24   **considered you . . .**

25 **BRIAN:** **Then I think you'd better start.** *(He starts advancing*

26   *toward her.)*

27 **KATHY:** *(Retreating)* **Brian!** *(She retreats to couch.)* **Look**

28   **Mr. Beansprouts, trying to mess up a perfect friendship**

29   **could be hazardous to your health.**

30 **BRIAN:** **You're right. But I'm willing to risk it.**

31 **KATHY:** *(As he continues to move in on her)* **Don't! Not a step**

32   **closer! OK, but don't say I didn't warn you.** *(She grabs a*

33   *Twinkee™ that is on a plate by the couch and jumps up onto the*

34   *cushions.)* **Back, back.** *(Disappointed)* **I thought a Twinkee**

35   **to you was the same as a cross is to Dracula.**

1　BRIAN:　Very funny. Now come here. *(He takes her by the shoulders*
2　　　　　*and is eye level or above.)* I want to go out with you. I don't
3　　　　　care what other people say. I don't have to prove anything
4　　　　　to them, and neither do you.
5　KATHY:　I know. It's just that . . . anytime I think about . . .
6　　　　　you and me, I laugh.
7　BRIAN:　*(Very close to her. Almost kissing. Beat)* I don't see you
8　　　　　laughing now.
9　KATHY:　That's because I'm not thinking. *(Pushing him away)*
10　　　　　Brian, we are not suited. I get up in the mornings and
11　　　　　have all I can do, to drink down my coffee. You get up
12　　　　　and drink raw eggs.
13　BRIAN:　Only when I'm in training.
14　KATHY:　You do? I can't. *(Gets off couch.)* Eating at a restaurant
15　　　　　that serves soybean burgers and cauliflower floats is not
16　　　　　my idea of fun. Besides, everyone will laugh at us.
17　BRIAN:　That's really it, isn't it? You're afraid of what people
18　　　　　will say.
19　KATHY:　No, no. That's not it at all. *(Walks away.)* Well, maybe
20　　　　　just a little bit of it. But mostly it's because of Rick. I
21　　　　　don't think I'm over him yet.
22　BRIAN:　*(He walks over to her and backs her against the wall. One*
23　　　　　*hand he places on the wall over her head)* Why don't you stop
24　　　　　thinking and start feeling? *(He kisses her and she pulls away.*
25　　　　　*She tries to move away and his other arm comes down and traps*
26　　　　　*her.)*
27　KATHY:　Brian don't. I don't think this is such . . . *(He kisses her*
28　　　　　*again, pushing her down to the floor. The camera watches them*
29　　　　　*as they slide out of sight — and we fade to black.)*
30
31
32
33
34
35

SCENE 27 — Yvonne and Stephen
Age Level 25-35

SCENE OPENS: STEPHEN and YVONNE are brother and sister.
YVONNE is pouring herself a drink at the bar. STEPHEN
walks in and sees her and stops. She senses his presence and
turns.

YVONNE: Don't look at me like that. *(Turns back to her drink.)*
You remind me of an old biddy with reproaches just
waiting to be said.

STEPHEN: And you remind me of an old drunkard with
nothing to lose but her self-respect.

YVONNE: Don't start, Stephen. I'm in no mood. *(She takes sip
and turns back to him, annoyed that he's still there.)* What do
you want?!

STEPHEN: For starters, I want you to stop drinking. I want
you to stop the pills. I want you to stop messing up your
life and start living again.

YVONNE: Oh, that. *(Turns back to the bar.)* Go away Stephen,
you're boring me.

STEPHEN: *(Beat)* Yvonne, I'm concerned about you.

YVONNE: Don't be. *(Turns back to him.)* Look, go busybody
yourself into someone else's life.

STEPHEN: Stop and listen to yourself. You sound like a tired,
old . . .

YVONNE: I am *not* old! Now how many ways do I have to say
this? I don't want you around me. You've turned into a
hovering, whiney old nanny and I can't stand it.

STEPHEN: You can say what you want, it doesn't hurt
anymore. What does hurt, is seeing you killing yourself.
(Grabs glass and wrenches it free.)

YVONNE: Give that back!

STEPHEN: No way. You want to drink yourself into an early
grave, you'll have to kill me first.

YVONNE: Don't tempt me. *(Beat)* Oh hell, keep the damn glass.

1   *(Grabs bottle.)* **I'll find another.** *(Turns to go.)*
2 **STEPHEN:**   **You don't get it, do you? There will be no more**
3   **glasses. At least not for you.**
4 **YVONNE:**   **What are you talking about?**
5 **STEPHEN:**   **Sit down, Yvonne. I'll go and make us some coffee.**
6 **YVONNE:**   **I don't want any coffee. And if I did, it certainly**
7   **wouldn't be with you.**
8 **STEPHEN:**   **You'd better sit down. I did a pretty mean tackle**
9   **at college and I'd hate to mess up your pretty party dress.**
10 **YVONNE:**   **You wouldn't dare.**
11 **STEPHEN:**   **Try me.** *(They stare at each other. Finally she sits.)*
12 **YVONNE:**   **All right. Say what you have to say and get it over**
13   **with.**
14 **STEPHEN:**   **First — I want you to know that I'm sorry, Yvonne.**
15 **YVONNE:**   **I'm touched.**
16 **STEPHEN:**   **Really sorry.**
17 **YVONNE:**   *(Turning to him. Slightly nervous)* **Sorry for what?**
18 **STEPHEN:**   **I've called the hospital. You're committed, as of**
19   **right now.**
20 **YVONNE:**   *(Stands)* **Jesus, Stephen!** *(Sees he's not lying. She goes*
21   *to phone and picks up.)* **Call them back and cancel.**
22 **STEPHEN:**   **Not this time. I'll go and make that coffee.**
23   *(STEPHEN exits.)*
24
25
26
27
28
29
30
31
32
33
34
35

SCENE 28 — Matthew and Kathryn

Age Level 30-55

SCENE OPENS: MATTHEW is a lawyer and has just arrived at
KATHRYN's house. He and his wife are friends of KATHRYN's
and her late husband. He is engaged in taking off his coat. He
places it on the back of the couch as he talks.

MATTHEW: Ellen sends her love. So — how has the widow
been?

KATHRYN: As good as can be expected. And my friend, the
lawyer? *(She smiles.)*

MATTHEW: Tired. I've been working long and hard on a
case. I'm beat.

KATHRYN: Let's hope not. *(They smile at joke.)* And to what do
I owe this honor?

MATTHEW: I was in the neighborhood and thought I'd drop
by. Between you, me and the lamppost, how are you really
doing?

KATHRYN: Fine. Lately, the dreams have stopped. I hope
this time it's forever.

MATTHEW: Give yourself a chance. It's not easy losing
someone you love.

KATHRYN: Right. You know Matt, if it hadn't been for you
and Ellen, I don't think I could have made it.

MATTHEW: Don't kid yourself. You're a pretty tough lady.
And besides, Charles was our friend too. People need to
grieve together, it seems to make the pain less.

KATHRYN: True. But that doesn't stop me from being very,
very grateful to you and Ellen. And it doesn't alter the
fact that I think you two are the best friends a person
could hope for in one lifetime.

MATTHEW: *(Goes to bar to fix a drink.)* So tell me, how's the rest
of your life?

KATHRYN: Coming along.

1	MATTHEW: *(Hears something in her voice and turns.)* **What is it**
2	**Kathryn? You can tell me.**
3	KATHRYN: **No I can't. I don't want you and Ellen sitting up**
4	**nights and holding my hand any longer.**
5	MATTHEW: **Is it serious? Do you need money?**
6	KATHRYN: **No, no. Nothing like that. It's ... I just miss**
7	**Charlie so much. I try not to think about him, but the**
8	**silliest things bring him to mind.**
9	MATTHEW: **I know. He was a very special guy. And you're a**
10	**very special woman who's got to start letting go of the**
11	**past.** *(He has taken her by the shoulders.)*
12	KATHRYN: *(Looking up at him)* **You're right. It must be terrible**
13	**to be right all of the ...** *(MATTHEW suddenly kisses her full*
14	*on the mouth. She pulls away shocked.)* **Matthew, what are**
15	**you doing?**
16	MATTHEW: **I thought that was obvious. I guess my timing was**
17	**off a bit.**
18	KATHRYN: **God Matthew! There shouldn't be that kind of**
19	**timing between us.**
20	MATTHEW: **Shouldn't is the key word. Look — I only did**
21	**what I've been wanting to do for a very long time.**
22	KATHRYN: **I don't believe I'm hearing this.**
23	MATTHEW: **Believe it.** *(Beat)* **Kathryn — I'm in love with you.**
24	**I've been in love with you for ...**
25	KATHRYN: **No! Don't you dare say any more.**
26	MATTHEW: **But I've got to. I'm in love with you and there**
27	**doesn't seem to be anything I can do about it. I never**
28	**wanted to tell you like this ...**
29	KATHRYN: **No more! If you don't have any feelings for how I**
30	**feel about what you're saying, at least think about Ellen.**
31	**Ellen ... oh God.** *(She sits.)*
32	MATTHEW: **Ellen and I are separated.**
33	KATHRYN: **Don't lie to me. I just talked to her yesterday, and**
34	**she didn't ...**
35	MATTHEW: **Ellen and I have been separated for two months**

1   now. We just didn't tell you. We felt that with all the stress

2   you were going through, we didn't want to add to it.

3   KATHRYN: I had no idea. Does she know why . . .

4   MATTHEW: No. But it's been coming for a long time now.

5   *(Sits down beside her.)* **Kathryn, I'm very sorry about how . . .**

6   KATHRYN: *(She gets up and moves away.)* **Matthew, I want you**

7   to go. I need to be alone.

8   MATTHEW: I understand. Telling you so soon was a mistake.

9   *(Gets up.)*

10   KATHRYN: Telling me at all was the mistake.

11   MATTHEW: *(Gathering coat)* I'll call you in a few weeks.

12   KATHRYN: No, not even in a few months. Matthew, I'm not a

13   psychiatrist but I think that perhaps because I needed

14   you and Ellen's so strong, that you might have confused

15   your feelings of friendship with love. You love Ellen and

16   I know that Ellen loves you.

17   MATTHEW: If you're trying to say that I don't know how I

18   feel or why, you're mistaken. Ellen and I were on the

19   verge of separating long before Charles died. In fact, I've

20   been in love with you . . .

21   KATHRYN: I don't think I can deal with this right now. I was

22   happy just being friends. Please, if we can, let's keep it

23   at that. OK?

24   MATTHEW: No, it's not OK. Not anymore. Kathryn, I want

25   you. I want you more than anything I've ever wanted in

26   my life. I'll give you some time to think about it, and then

27   I'm going to call. And I'll keep calling until you answer.

28   KATHRYN: Don't do that. You don't know what you're saying.

29   MATTHEW: Don't confuse with me Charles. I always know

30   what I'm saying and I always know what I want. *(Goes to*

31   *the door and turns back to her.)* I want you. And I usually

32   get what I want. *(MATTHEW exits.)*

33

34

35

SCENE 29 — Curt and Rita

Age Level 20-40

SCENE OPENS: CURT and RITA have been friends for most of their lives. They enter with CURT walking before RITA.

CURT: No matter how many times you ask me, I'm not going to tell you.

RITA: But why? I've told you so many secrets about my life. I don't see any reason why you should hold out on me.

CURT: Because I don't feel like telling you, that's why.

RITA: I'm not going to tell anybody, if that's what you're afraid of. Your secret will die with me.

CURT: If you don't stop nagging me — you're going to be the one who'll die.

RITA: What's the big deal? So you're in love with someone. People fall in love every day.

CURT: Not this people. I never should have told you in the first place.

RITA: Why not? Come on, what could it hurt?

CURT: It could hurt . . . look Rita, she doesn't know how I feel and . . . I don't think she'd be too happy about it.

RITA: Then she would be a total fool. *(Beat)* Why wouldn't she be happy about it?

CURT: It's too complicated to explain. And that's as far as I'm going to go. End of discussion.

RITA: Curtis Malloy — you'd better tell me who this mystery woman is — or suffer the consequences.

CURT: What consequences? Don't tell me you'll stop talking to me. Oh gee Rita, I don't think I could stand five minutes of silence.

RITA: Very funny. I really think this is important enough to share. And you're not abiding by our rules.

CURT: Rita, we were twelve years old when we made up those silly rules. That was a long time ago.

1   RITA: I didn't realize that time could erode a sworn pact of
2   blood. A promise. A lifelong bound that . . .
3   CURT: I can't tell you. You'll just have to trust me on this. OK?
4   RITA: *(Relenting)* **Oh, all right.** *(She sits on couch.)*
5   CURT: **Truce?** *(Holds out hand.)*
6   RITA: *(Shaking hands)* **Temporarily.**
7   CURT: **By the way,** *(Walks behind a chair)* **I can't make our**
8   **date on Thursday.** *(Seeing her face)* **I'm sorry, but**
9   **something came up and I can't go.**
10   RITA: *(Goes to chair and kneels on it.)* **Curt, in all seriousness,**
11   **have I done something to upset you? This is the fourth**
12   **date you've cancelled on me.**
13   CURT: **I know and I'm sorry. Rita, you know I'd rather be**
14   **out with you than anyone I know. It's just . . .**
15   RITA: **Actually, that's not true anymore, is it? Your mystery**
16   **woman probably takes top billing now.**
17   CURT: **No, not really. It's painful to be around her. I try to**
18   **avoid it.** *(Walks around and sits down on couch.)*
19   RITA: *(Contrite)* **Oh Curt, I'm sorry. I've been very childish**
20   **and inconsiderate.**
21   CURT: *(Lightly)* **The very qualities that make you so alluring.**
22   **I guess you can take Charles Fenter to that party. He's**
23   **rich and he's crazy about you. You deserve the best.**
24   RITA: **Charles is the best all right. Best at being boring,**
25   **tedious and . . . squirmy.** *(Shudders)*
26   CURT: **At least he has money. I think you said, and correct**
27   **me if I'm misquoting you, "You can forgive a person**
28   **almost everything, if he's rich".**
29   RITA: **When I said that — I obviously hadn't met Charles yet.**
30   *(Beat)* **Is that why you've been avoiding me?**
31   CURT: **I haven't been avoiding you. But it stands to reason,**
32   **if you hang out with me, how will you meet anybody else?**
33   RITA: **I like hanging out with you. You're my friend.**
34   CURT: **Maybe we should think about seeing less of each**
35   **other. It does cramp both our social lives.**

1	RITA:	*(Goes to couch and sits beside him.)* **Don't say that. You're**
2		**the best friend I have in the world. I love you Curt.**
3	CURT:	**And I love you too Rita. We'll always be friends.**
4	RITA:	*(Impulsively she hugs him.)* **You're such a great guy. I**
5		**wish you would tell your mystery woman how you feel.**
6		**You could be surprised. She may be interested in you too.**
7	CURT:	**I don't think so.** *(Gets up and moves away.)*
8	RITA:	*(Following him)* **Listen to me Curt. Nothing ventured,**
9		**nothing gained. Love doesn't come every single day. If**
10		**you really care about her, you've got to let her know**
11		**about it.**
12	CURT:	**No I don't. She wouldn't want to hear me say it. It**
13		**would spoil things. Make her unhappy.**
14	RITA:	**How could telling someone you love them, make them**
15		**unhappy?**
16	CURT:	*(Angry)* **Take my word for it Rita! I know.**
17	RITA:	*(Beat)* **Sorry.** *(Starts to gather coat.)* **I should mind my**
18		**own business, shouldn't I? Me and my big mouth. I never**
19		**know when to shut up.**
20	CURT:	*(Stopping her)* **Rita, I'm sorry. It's just that I can't tell**
21		**her, just like I can't tell you who it is.** *(Cups her face with*
22		*his hand.)* **Come on, don't look so depressed. One secret**
23		**in the many years we've been friends isn't too bad, is it?**
24	RITA:	**No, I guess not.** *(They stare at each other and CURT slowly*
25		*draws forward to kiss her. Surprised, she pulls away.)* **I think**
26		**I should be going.**
27	CURT:	*(Walks away from her.)* **Rita . . .** *(Embarrassed)* **I don't**
28		**know what came over me. Must be fatigue.**
29	RITA:	**I . . . there's no need to apologize.**
30	CURT:	**I shouldn't have . . .**
31	RITA:	**Isn't that funny? How in the twinkling of an instant,**
32		**things can change.**
33	CURT:	**Rita don't . . .**
34	RITA:	**You're not my friend anymore.**
35	CURT:	**Please don't say any more. I understand.**

1   RITA: No — you don't understand. And I think I've just
2   discovered who your mystery woman might be. *(She goes*
3   *to him and they embrace.)*
4
5
6
7
8
9
10
11
12
13
14
15
16
17
18
19
20
21
22
23
24
25
26
27
28
29
30
31
32
33
34
35

SCENE 30 — Roxanne and Gary
Age Level 25-35

SCENE OPENS: ROXANNE is a newswoman. GARY and she have
   been married for a year. ROXANNE is fixing her pearls in the
   mirror and is dressed to go out. GARY enters.

GARY: Going somewhere?

ROXANNE: Oh. Yes.

GARY: You *do* remember that we've got a party to go to
   tonight.

ROXANNE: Yep.

GARY: When will you be back?

ROXANNE: I'll meet you there.

GARY: You know I hate to go to parties alone. Especially
   when I don't know anybody.

ROXANNE: This is important Gary. You know I wouldn't do
   it if it wasn't.

GARY: No I don't. Lately, you've been doing this a lot.

ROXANNE: Sorry, but I've got to. *(Sees him reflected in mirror.)*
   Don't look so woebegone. I'll get there around nine. We'll
   have a good time.

GARY: You said that last time and you didn't even show. If I
   had known you weren't going with me tonight, I would
   have made other plans.

ROXANNE: Don't be a pain, Gary. OK?

GARY: Now I'm a pain? Thanks! *(Goes to leave.)*

ROXANNE: Gary. *(He turns back.)* In another week or so, this
   will all be over. In the meantime, you'll just have to be
   patient. OK?

GARY: No it's not OK. Not this time.

ROXANNE: Stop acting like a baby. My job calls for unusual
   hours. You knew that before we even got married.

GARY: You call "out all night" unusual hours? I call them
   cheating hours. I call them "to hell with this marriage" hours.

1   ROXANNE: What?

2   GARY: You heard me.

3   ROXANNE: This is ridiculous! I'm at the very end of winding
4   up the biggest story of my career, and you're ranting and
5   raving about cheating? I haven't had the time to think
6   about cheating let alone do it!

7   GARY: It's not the thinking part, I'm worried about.

8   ROXANNE: *(Goes to him.)* Oh honey, let's not . . .

9   GARY: *(Pushing her away)* Don't oh honey me. I want my wife
10   back. I want to go to dinner with a companion not a
11   newspaper. I want to show up at parties as a couple, not
12   stag. I'm sick of it and I want it to stop.

13   ROXANNE: Listen to you. I want. I want. What about me?
14   Or us? This job can mean so much to us, if I can . . .

15   GARY: Don't try that. It won't work. As far as I'm concerned,
16   you gave *us* up when you took on this assignment.

17   ROXANNE: You're talking nonsense. We both agreed that
18   this was a fantastic opportunity. It just requires more
19   time away from each other than we thought. I don't like
20   it anymore than you do.

21   GARY: I bet you don't. Cocktail parties till 3 a.m. Jet setting
22   to the islands . . .

23   ROXANNE: Look — I would be lying if I said I didn't enjoy
24   myself. But while they're fun things *(Moves in to him)*
25   they're done without you. That makes the difference. It
26   isn't the same kind of enjoyment I'd have if you were
27   there with me.

28   GARY: *(Doesn't respond)* I'm touched.

29   ROXANNE: *(Exasperated)* Why are you acting like this? Next
30   week everything will be back to normal and this will all
31   be history.

32   GARY: *(Walks to door and turns.)* You think so? If you don't go
33   to this party with me . . . you can consider our relationship
34   history. *(GARY exits.)*

35

SCENE 31 — John and Susan

Age Level 25-40

SCENE OPENS: JOHN and SUSAN are brother-in-law and sister-in-law. SUSAN is staring out the window as JOHN enters, stops and watches her for a minute. He then approaches, bringing her a drink.

JOHN: Sure is quiet without everybody else around, isn't it?

SUSAN: It's lovely. *(Awkward pause)* **John, do you ever want to escape? Ever want to leave and never come back?**

JOHN: There isn't a day goes by that I don't think about it at least once.

SUSAN: I always thought I would die before I went to Hell. *(Goes and sits on couch.)* **How do you stand it?**

JOHN: Oh, you get used to it. *(Following her)* **It's like living on a battlefield where no one wins or loses. Both sides just keep on fighting.**

SUSAN: That's what this family reminds me of. A country under siege. *(Lightly. As making a joke)* **Bomb squads. Land mines. But worst of all, their ghoulish faces pressed up against the window panes, gloating over the destruction and counting up the dead and dying.**

JOHN: I didn't realize they'd finally gotten to you. *(Beat)* **If you want my advice, you should leave right now. Pack up your bags and go. With or without Doug.**

SUSAN: *(Gets up and moves away.)* **He's my husband. I can't leave him.**

JOHN: Can't? Or won't.

SUSAN: If I left — he'd have no one. Nothing.

JOHN: He'd cope. Douglas is a lot stronger than you give him credit for.

SUSAN: I promised I wouldn't leave. I promised and I'm not going back on my word.

JOHN: When you promised — did you know it was going to

1   **be like this?** *(Beat. She turns away from him.)* **I didn't think so.**

2   SUSAN: *(Turns back to him.)* **Why don't you go? What keeps**
3   **you here?**

4   JOHN: *(Gets up and walks slowly to her.)* **Living in it for so long,**
5   **I guess I'm afraid of what else is out there. You get**
6   **comfortable. Even with pain.**

7   SUSAN: **You're settling for misery when you could achieve**
8   **so much.**

9   JOHN: **Like what?**

10   SUSAN: **Writing. You have a wonderful talent for writing.**
11   **Why don't you try and do something with it.**

12   JOHN: **Oh? You mean write sentimental pap for mushy**
13   **greeting cards? Or perhaps amusing predictions in**
14   **Chinese fortune cookies.** *(Takes deep sip from glass.)*

15   SUSAN: **You sound like Douglas. You deserve better than**
16   **that from yourself.**

17   JOHN: *(Angry)* **How do you know? How do you know so much,**
18   **Miss Know-it-All?**

19   SUSAN: **John don't.** *(Turns away.)*

20   JOHN: *(Goes up to her. Over the shoulder)* **Don't what? Don't tell**
21   **you when you're being condescending?** *(Grabs her elbow*
22   *and turns her around to face him.)* **Let me tell you something.**
23   **It's all anyone can do to survive in this family, let alone**
24   **try and reach for a dream.** *(Lets go and walks away.)* **And**
25   **that's all my writing is. A dream.**

26   SUSAN: **You could make it a reality. You could . . .**

27   JOHN: **Oh, that's rich. You telling me what to do. Actions**
28   **speak louder than words, and all I see is your sorry self,**
29   **still stuck in this family — just like me. And don't try and**
30   **pretty up your reasons for staying. Self-sacrifice, like hell.**
31   **You're here for the money and** *(Toasts with glass)* **the**
32   **bowing and scraping that goes with the exalted name.**
33   **Admit it.**

34   SUSAN: *(Beat)* **I don't deserve that. Not from you.** *(She puts*
35   *down glass, and starts to leave.)*

```
1   JOHN:   Susan . . . (She stops. The rest he says with an apologetic
2           drawl.) this ol' gunslinger is just overtired and (Makes his
3           finger like a gun) shootin' at shadows.
4   SUSAN:   Right partner. (Takes finger and shoots back.) Just
5           shootin' at shadows. (Pause. SUSAN exits.)
6
7
8
9
10
11
12
13
14
15
16
17
18
19
20
21
22
23
24
25
26
27
28
29
30
31
32
33
34
35
```

SCENE 32 — Chris and Holly
Age Level 18-28

SCENE OPENS: CHRIS and HOLLY are stepbrother and stepsister. They've just had a fight about Evan and HOLLY asked CHRIS to leave. CHRIS is sitting in HOLLY's living room. She comes in and sees him.

HOLLY: What are you doing here? I thought I told you to go home.

CHRIS: You did. But I didn't.

HOLLY: Chris — I don't want you butting into my life any longer. You've got to quit it.

CHRIS: *(Gets up.)* A brother's responsibility never quits.

HOLLY: This stepbrother . . . *(Walks to him)* had better quit.

CHRIS: I take my responsibilities seriously, Holly. One can never be too careful you know.

HOLLY: Look — I appreciate your concern, I really do, but — you're driving me nuts!

CHRIS: Me? Why? Because I don't like Evan? Because I think you could do better if you were blindfolded and picked a name out of a prison register?

HOLLY: Stop it.

CHRIS: Stop what?

HOLLY: You know what! Keep your opinions of Evan to yourself. What do you have against him, anyway?

CHRIS: Absolutely nothing. *(Turns and as he walks to couch and sits)* It's just that he's a zero. I don't understand what you see in him.

HOLLY: I see a warm, sensitive . . . fascinating man.

CHRIS: Just goes to show how blind love can be.

HOLLY: I am begging you, Chris. *(Goes to couch and sits.)* Leave us alone. And if you're right and I am making a mistake — then let *me* make it.

CHRIS: If I can stop you from hurting yourself, why shouldn't I?

1   People who care about other people should be able to
2   protect them, shouldn't they?
3 HOLLY: Yes and no. Sometimes people have to find out
4   things the hard way. *(Takes his hand.)* Love me enough
5   for that. OK?
6 CHRIS: *(Beat)* OK. *(As she goes to get up)* But don't say I didn't
7   warn you.
8 HOLLY: I won't *(Goes to kitchen door.)* Thanks.
9 CHRIS: *(As HOLLY starts to leave)* But if you need a shoulder
10   to cry on . . . I'll be here.
11 HOLLY: Right. Love ya pal.
12 CHRIS: Love you too.
13 HOLLY: *(Hesitates at door.)* Chris, I was thinking — are you
14   doing anything tonight?
15 CHRIS: No. Why? *(Gets up.)*
16 HOLLY: Because I thought that maybe you could come over
17   for dinner. Kind of like a fresh start for both of us. What
18   do you say?
19 CHRIS: I say — *(Excited)* OK! We'll make it just like old times.
20   I'll bring the popcorn.
21 HOLLY: Great! This way you can really get to know Evan.
22 CHRIS: You mean Evan will be here?
23 HOLLY: Yes. I thought . . . do you still have a problem with
24   that?
25 CHRIS: No. No problem. But I just remembered that I have
26   an appointment tonight and can't make it. Maybe some
27   other time.
28 HOLLY: Chris, you promised.
29 CHRIS: No I didn't. I said I'd try to stay out of your business.
30   That doesn't mean I have to socialize with him.
31 HOLLY: At least give it a try. I'm sure once you get to know
32   Evan you'll like him.
33 CHRIS: Oh. Now I'm supposed to like him? Look Holly — if
34   you want to spend your time with a low life like Evan —
35   go ahead. But don't expect me to like it and don't expect

1   me to participate. All right! *(CHRIS heads for outer door.)*
2 HOLLY: Don't go. I'm sorry. I don't mean to push Evan on
3   you. It's just that both of you mean so much to me — I
4   want you guys to be friends.
5 CHRIS: Face it Holly. It will be a cold day in Hell before I
6   become friends with Evan. *(Beat)* Give me a call when
7   you're free. *(Gives her a kiss on the cheek.)* I'll see you later
8   sis. *(CHRIS exits.)*

SCENE 33 — Jason and Maria

Age Level 17-28

SCENE OPENS: JASON is holding a gift-wrapped package that MARIA has given him. Through till end, JASON is very matter of fact.

JASON: *(Looking at gift)* **Why'd you do this, Maria? You're making this so much more difficult than it has to be.**

MARIA: **It's your birthday. And I wanted to make sure this was the first year someone gave you a gift.**

JASON: **You could have sent it by mail.**

MARIA: **I know. But I wanted to hear you tell me again — this time in person — why I'm supposed to forget *us*.**

JASON: **We already went over it on the phone. Look — it's not going to come out any more gently with you staring at me like that.** *(Walks away.)* **Why can't you just accept it and go home?**

MARIA: *(Walks up behind him.)* **Because I know you love me.**

JASON: *(Turns to her.)* **This is the last time I'm gonna say it! I don't.** *(Throws gift down on couch.)*

MARIA: **Why? What's changed you?**

JASON: **Nothing. I just need some space and I don't want you hanging around any longer, that's all.**

MARIA: **Jason, who's making you say this? Gordon?**

JASON: **Your brother has nothing to do with it. Maria —** *(Takes her by shoulders)* **you're a sweet girl and someday you're going to make someone very happy — but that someone is not going to be me.**

MARIA: **Are you telling me you lied?** *(JASON walks away from her.)* **All those nights? About everything?**

JASON: *(His back to her.)* **Every single word was a lie.** *(Turning back)* **Satisfied?**

MARIA: *(Beat)* **You ... you couldn't have ...**

JASON: **I did. Welcome to the real world, Maria. I just wasn't**

1	thinking about you or how you would feel. I was interested
2	in me and how to get what I wanted. Sorry, but that's the
3	kind of guy I am.
4	MARIA: All the secret things we shared? They were lies too?
5	JASON: Yes!
6	MARIA: But ... you cried when you told me about your
7	mother dying and ... I don't believe you! *(Turns away.)*
8	JASON: *(Going up behind her. Over the shoulder shot)* You'd
9	better — because it's the truth.
10	MARIA: Jason *(Turning back)* you're describing someone I
11	don't know. Someone I never knew.
12	JASON: You're beginning to get the picture. Call me what
13	you want. Louse. Bum. Rat. They're all true. And believe
14	it or not, I feel really crummy about this.
15	MARIA: Crummy?! *You* feel crummy?!
16	JASON: *(Awkward pause)* I've got to get ready to go. I'm late
17	enough as it is. *(Opens door and starts to hussle her out. Extends*
18	*his hand.)* Let's just call it quits and continue to be friends.
19	OK babe?
20	MARIA: *(Doesn't take hand)* Friends? You no longer exist for
21	me Jason. Not now. Not ever! You got that straight, *babe*?
22	JASON: At least I'm being honest about who I am.
23	MARIA: *(Claps hands slowly.)* Well ... good ... for ... you!
24	Don't bother to return the gift. Keep it as a souvenir for
25	that — honesty. *(Exits)*
26	JASON: *(Beat. Slowly goes to gift and picks up. Closes fist over it.)*
27	Damn you Gordon. If it's the last thing I do — I'm gonna
28	get you for this. I swear I am. On my mother's grave.
29	
30	
31	
32	
33	
34	
35	

SCENE 34 — Bill and Sara

Age Level 16-19

SCENE OPENS: BILL and SARA are in living room with a bottle
of champagne.

BILL: *(Pops cork.)* **A celebration. To graduation. And — to us.**
(Pouring)

SARA: **To us!** *(Takes sip.)* **Ummmm. This is good.**

BILL: *(Snuggles up.)* ***Life*** **is good. And this has got to be the
best year of our lives. Wanna know why?**

SARA: **You love me.**

BILL: **Yep. And . . .**

SARA: **And you can't live without me.**

BILL: **And . . .**

SARA: **And . . . when you have kids you want them to have
my eyes.** *(Smiles up at him.)*

BILL: **This is much bigger, Sara.**

SARA: **What do you mean bigger?!**

BILL: **I mean more immediate. Like in a few months.**

SARA: **Actually, I have some immediate news myself. But
you go first.**

BILL: *(Gets up.)* **OK.** *(Lifts glass.)* **To you. To me and . . . to
St. Francis.**

SARA: **St. Francis?**

BILL: **They accepted me. Isn't that great?!**

SARA: **Yeah. Great.** *(Puts down glass.)*

BILL: **Look — I know we'd planned on getting married right
away, but it's a *full* scholarship.**

SARA: **I'm happy for you Bill, really. But . . .**

BILL: **You know you can't get anywhere in life without a
college education.**

SARA: **You said you didn't care about college. You'd make it
on your own, like Louie.**

BILL: **That was before I got the scholarship. Besides, Louie**

1   works at a garage.

2   SARA: What's wrong with a garage? He makes good money.

3   BILL: Sara, it's a dead end. He can't go anywhere from there.

4   Baby this is a chance . . .

5   SARA: A chance for what? For you to break your promises?

6   To find someone new? *(Wrenches free.)* **Never mind.** *(Gets*

7   *up.)* **Congratulations!** *(Turns away.)*

8   BILL: *(Goes up behind her.)* **Awwww, come on Sara. I love you. I**

9   thought you'd be happy for me. It just means putting off

10   marriage a couple of years, that's all.

11   SARA: A couple of . . . *(Turns to him)* it's not that simple Bill.

12   BILL: Then make it that simple. At least our parents will be

13   thrilled.

14   SARA: I don't think so.

15   BILL: Sure they will. You told me yourself how your mom

16   went nuts when you told her our plans.

17   SARA: That was then.

18   BILL: Hey — she's only looked into a few reception halls. It's

19   not like she put any money down. As far as she's

20   concerned, you're still too young with your whole life

21   ahead of you. At least you guys can quit fighting about

22   it now. Sara — this is an opportunity for *us.*

23   SARA: No Bill. Not for us.

24   BILL: *(Pulls away angry.)* **Jeez, I don't understand you Sara.**

25   A husband without a college degree is a man who can

26   look at life pass him by. How much could I expect to make

27   a year? You want to end up like your mom? Screaming

28   kids — old before you're forty?

29   SARA: No! But sometimes you don't get a choice.

30   BILL: That's what I'm trying to tell ya. An education can give

31   us that choice. *(Goes and hugs her.)* **Hey cheer up. Everything**

32   will work out OK. You'll see. Now — what was the good

33   news you wanted to tell me.?

34   SARA: *(Beat)* **I don't remember.** *(Picks up champagne glass.)* **To the**

35   best year of our lives! *(They clink glasses. Close out on SARA)*

SCENE 35 — Jim and Carly

Age Level 20-35

SCENE OPENS: CARLY and JIM are in restaurant.

JIM: Why can't it be right now?

CARLY: It's too complicated to explain. Look — *you* need to leave town tonight. Brad's going to find out if you stay any longer.

JIM: So let him.

CARLY: Easy for you to say. You're not married to him.

JIM: You don't have to be either. Come with me, Carly. Just walk away from him.

CARLY: He'd find me.

JIM: So? You'd tell him you're staying with me. And that would be the end of it.

CARLY: *(Smiles)* You don't know him like I do.

JIM: I don't need to. You don't have to do anything you don't want to. Got it? I'll flatten old Brad into a pancake if he tries anything.

CARLY: He wouldn't try anything obvious like physical violence. He's much more subtle.

JIM: I'm impervious to subtle.

CARLY: You weren't impervious to the six months down in Chester Prison.

JIM: *(Beat)* Are you saying that Brad was behind my frame up?

CARLY: Let's just say he's real good friends with Sergeant Dickerson, who's chummy with Mike Stratford.

JIM: Why that low, sleezy . . .

CARLY: Doesn't mean he was behind it — it just means you've got to be more careful. He's got friends everywhere.

JIM: I think it means Brad's gonna have to be more careful. Now I definitely owe him one.

CARLY: Jim, look at me. I only told you that because you underestimate Brad. That's a dangerous mistake to make.

1 JIM: Looks like Brad and I have both made some mistakes.

2 CARLY: Let it go. Forget it and get on with your life.

3 JIM: Forget it? Six months in jail, a record to boot and you
4   want me to shrug it off?!

5 CARLY: I'm afraid for you, Jim. You've got to lay low for a
6   while and stay there. Here, *(She shoves envelope at him)* this
7   should help.

8 JIM: What's this?

9 CARLY: Just a little something I managed to put aside. Some
10   dream money. Take it and go.

11 JIM: I'm not going without you.

12 CARLY: *(Looking nervously around)* Maybe later. *(Sees JIM
13   watching her.)* It's no use trying to get me to go with you
14   now. I can't and that's all there is to it.

15 JIM: I'm a little confused. You hate him. You're afraid of him.
16   You're husband and wife in name only. What's keeping
17   you here?

18 CARLY: I have my reasons. *(Angry)* And I don't have to explain
19   them to you.

20 JIM: Oh, no? I love you damn it! And you love me. I'm not
21   leaving without some sort of explanation.

22 CARLY: *(Beat)* All right. He . . . he found out I'm pregnant.

23 JIM: You're what?! Oh Carly honey . . . *(He takes her hand.)*

24 CARLY: *(Pulls hand away.)* It's not yours, so don't get excited.
25   Anyway — Brad and I — well one night we . . .

26 JIM: You made love to Brad?

27 CARLY: He has his ways of getting what he wants. I told you,
28   you don't really know him.

29 JIM: *(Beat)* Actually — it looks as though I don't really know
30   *you.* *(Looks at envelope. Throws it at her.)* Here, keep it. The
31   way you live lady, you need more dream money than I
32   do. *(Exits)*

33 CARLY: *(Watches him go. Picks up envelope. To self)* Isn't it
34   funny? To get dream money, one has to live a nightmare.
35   *(Puts money in bag. Takes wine glass and takes long drink.)*

SCENE 36 — Jesse and Clara

Age Level 16-20

SCENE OPENS: JESSE and CLARA are outside under a tree. They love each other but they are both quick tempered, which keeps them apart.

JESSE: How much of what I heard is true? *(Roughly grabs her arm.)* How much?!

CLARA: *(Wrenches free.)* Don't manhandle me! And Jesse Smith if you want to know something — why don't you just ask nice.

JESSE: *(Beat)* I heard . . . you're planning on marrying Greg.

CLARA: Who told you that?

JESSE: Is it true?

CLARA: I haven't gotten any other offers lately.

JESSE: *(Beat)* Did you say yes?

CLARA: I told him I'd think about it. He loves me.

JESSE: Ha! The only person Greg cares about is himself. You would just make a nice addition to his "collection".

CLARA: That's not true. You only hate him because he likes me — and because he's rich.

JESSE: He's only rich because his daddy stole my father's invention. If he thinks . . .

CLARA: *(Over him)* Oh Jesse, we're not going to hear that again, are we? So your father showed his ideas to a friend, and that friend doubled-crossed him. It happens all the time.

JESSE: It happens . . . ! You didn't have to watch your father shrivel up and die, because his dream was stolen.

CLARA: Jess — if you keep living in the past, your future will slip through your fingers. *(Moving close to him and pressing up against his side)* Not to mention the present.

JESSE: *(Unmoved)* This how you act when you're out with Greg?

1	CLARA:	Ohh! *(Smacking him)* **You're making me crazy!** *(Starts*
2		*to go.)*
3	JESSE:	**Answer me! Wait Clara.** *(Goes to her.)* **I'm sorry. When I**
4		**think of Greg and you together — I can't think of**
5		**anything except my hate.**
6	CLARA:	**You frighten me, Jess. You get so steamed and angry**
7		**that you don't hear or see people as they are.** *(Moves away.)*
8		**Just what you imagine.**
9	JESSE:	**I'm trying to change like you asked me, Clara. But**
10		**. . .** *(Thoughtful)* **that lousy family fills my mind and**
11		**sometimes I get so mad, I feel like I can't breathe. Like**
12		**I'm gonna explode.**
13	CLARA:	*(Walks to him.)* **I know Jess, it's hard to let go. But you**
14		**need to start trusting people. Like me. I won't do anything**
15		**to hurt you.** *(She puts hand on his cheek and draws him into a kiss.)*
16	JESSE:	**You kiss Greg like that?** *(She pulls sharply away.)* **I**
17		**didn't mean . . .**
18	CLARA:	**That does it! You're so obsessed with Greg, I wonder**
19		**if you go out with me just to get even with him.**
20	JESSE:	**What are you talking about?**
21	CLARA:	*(Whipping herself into a frenzy)* **You know — that's not**
22		**such a crazy idea. Greg started going out with me** *before*
23		**you even gave me a second look.**
24	JESSE:	**That's not true! I liked you long before Greg ever**
25		**asked you out. Only I made the stupid mistake of telling**
26		**people. He must have heard and decided to steal something**
27		**else from the Smiths.**
28	CLARA:	**Steal something else?! Is that what I am to you? A**
29		**thing to be stolen?**
30	JESSE:	**That's not what I meant.**
31	CLARA:	**It's what you said.**
32	JESSE:	**You're blowing this whole thing out of proportion.**
33	CLARA:	**No I'm not. I just realized this entire competitive**
34		**game you're playing with Greg, involves me. You don't**
35		**feel anything for me. It's just another way to get at Greg!**

1	JESSE:	Not true! I care about you very . . .

1   JESSE: Not true! I care about you very . . .
2   CLARA: Care? Well, that in itself says a lot, doesn't it? Greg
3   told me he *loved* me. Seems to be a whole jump ahead of
4   you this time, Jess.
5   JESSE: Clara — don't you start too.
6   CLARA: I'm not starting anything. In fact, I'm finishing it.
7   Good-bye and good riddance to you Jesse Smith. Come
8   and see me and my new husband when you get the
9   chance. You hear? *(Starts to go.)*
10   JESSE: Now you're the one going crazy. Come here, Clara.
11   *(She pulls away.)* Come on, calm down.
12   CLARA: Calm down yourself! After I'm married, maybe then
13   you'll come around to finding out you love me. 'Course,
14   you'll be too late. But then you know what they say Jess —
15   "Like father, like son". *(CLARA exits.)*
16
17
18
19
20
21
22
23
24
25
26
27
28
29
30
31
32
33
34
35

ABOUT THE AUTHOR

Karen S. Dent is presently head writer for New Roads Productions in Los Angeles, California, producers of a new soap opera for teenagers. She is also a professional actress on call for roles in network soaps, commercials, industrial films and off-off Broadway shows.

She comes from a theatrical family. Her father (deceased) is listed in *Who's Who in American Theatre* and her mother is an ex-actress, editor and published author. Her sister has published seven novels. Karen toured with her parents as a child, often being carried on stage when her parents did scenes from the classics for educational institutions.

Her considerable talent has been honed and expanded by association with many of the finest professionals in TV, theatre and stage.

ORDER FORM

MERIWETHER PUBLISHING LTD.
P.O. BOX 7710
COLORADO SPRINGS, CO 80933
TELEPHONE: (719) 594-4422

Please send me the following books:

_____ **The Soaps — Scene Stealing Scenes for Actors** $9.95
by **Karen Dent** **#TT-B123**
36 professional level soap opera scenes for acting practice

_____ **TV Scenes for Actors #TT-B137** $14.95
by **Sigmund A. Stoler**
Selected short scenes from the Golden Age of TV Drama

_____ **Encore! More Winning Monologs for Young** $7.95
Actors #TT-B144
by **Peg Kehret**
More honest-to-life monologs for young actors

_____ **Winning Monologs for Young Actors #TT-B127** $7.95
by **Peg Kehret**
Honest-to-life monologs for young actors

_____ **Two Character Plays for Student Actors #TT-B174** $7.95
by **Robert Mauro**
A collection of 15 one-act plays

_____ **Original Audition Scenes for Actors #TT-B129** $9.95
by **Garry Michael Kluger**
A book of professional-level dialogs and monologs

_____ **57 Original Auditions for Actors #TT-B181** $6.95
by **Eddie Lawrence**
A workbook of monologs for actors

I understand that I may return any book
for a full refund if not satisfied.

NAME: _____

ORGANIZATION NAME: _____

ADDRESS: _____

CITY: _____ STATE: _____ ZIP: _____

PHONE: _____

☐ **Check Enclosed**
☐ **Visa or Master Card #**_____

Signature: _____
(required for Visa/Mastercard orders)

COLORADO RESIDENTS: Please add 3% sales tax.
SHIPPING: Include $1.50 for the first book and 50¢ for each additional book ordered.

☐ *Please send me a copy of your complete catalog of books or plays.*

ORDER FORM

MERIWETHER PUBLISHING LTD.
P.O. BOX 7710
COLORADO SPRINGS, CO 80933
TELEPHONE: (719) 594-4422

Please send me the following books:

_____**The Soaps — Scene Stealing Scenes for Actors** **$9.95**
by **Karen Dent #TT-B123**
36 professional level soap opera scenes for acting practice

_____**TV Scenes for Actors #TT-B137** **$14.95**
by **Sigmund A. Stoler**
Selected short scenes from the Golden Age of TV Drama

_____**Encore! More Winning Monologs for Young** **$7.95**
Actors #TT-B144
by **Peg Kehret**
More honest-to-life monologs for young actors

_____**Winning Monologs for Young Actors #TT-B127** **$7.95**
by **Peg Kehret**
Honest-to-life monologs for young actors

_____**Two Character Plays for Student Actors #TT-B174** **$7.95**
by **Robert Mauro**
A collection of 15 one-act plays

_____**Original Audition Scenes for Actors #TT-B129** **$9.95**
by **Garry Michael Kluger**
A book of professional-level dialogs and monologs

_____**57 Original Auditions for Actors #TT-B181** **$6.95**
by **Eddie Lawrence**
A workbook of monologs for actors

> *I understand that I may return any book*
> *for a full refund if not satisfied.*

NAME: _____

ORGANIZATION NAME: _____

ADDRESS: _____

CITY: _____ STATE: _____ ZIP: _____

PHONE: _____

☐ **Check Enclosed**
☐ **Visa or Master Card #**_____

Signature: _____
(required for Visa/Mastercard orders)

COLORADO RESIDENTS: Please add 3% sales tax.
SHIPPING: Include $1.50 for the first book and 50¢ for each additional book ordered.

☐ *Please send me a copy of your complete catalog of books or plays.*